The social history of Canada

MICHAEL BLISS, EDITOR

A STUDY OF CITY CONDITIONS

A PLEA FOR SOCIAL SERVICE

My neighbor

J. S. WOODSWORTH

WITH AN INTRODUCTION BY RICHARD ALLEN

UNIVERSITY OF TORONTO PRESS

© University of Toronto Press 1972
Toronto and Buffalo
ISBN (casebound) 0-8020-1824-6
ISBN (paperback) 0-8020-6126-5
Microfiche ISBN 0-8020-0144-0
LC 77-163839
Printed in the United States of America

An introduction

BY RICHARD ALLEN

'IN CANADA, the city and its problems are only beginning to require serious consideration, 'wrote J. S. Woodsworth in 1909.[1] An observer of the 1970s might comment with too much truth that the city and its problems are only now beginning to receive the attention they merited half a century before. In 1911 Woodsworth went on to write *My Neighbor,* a pioneering study of Canadian civic pathology and an impassioned plea for urban reform. Despite the problems of the city under the double impact of industrialization and immigration, he was able to write with considerable optimism. Ironically and tragically, the sprouting urban consciousness which he observed, and did his best to nurture, was soon to be stunted by an overgrowth of provincial and national concerns.

At the time that Woodsworth wrote, the budgets of the three largest Canadian cities were roughly equal to those of the provinces in which they were situated. However, the waging of two wars, overcoming a prolonged depression, the making of a welfare state, forging a universal public education system, and the maintenance of national unity all conspired to augment national and provincial status and displace the burgeoning concern for the emerging city. More recently, continuing urban growth, prolonged prosperity, an enlarged sense of the ecological interdependence of man and nature, renewed concern for the quality of life, and a flowering of the arts, despite budgets which no longer rival those of the provinces, have reawakened the early century's consciousness of the city. With remarkable contemporaneity, Woodsworth speaks across the half-century eclipse of the Canadian city.

Both the lapsing and the renewal of urban consciousness makes the reprinting of *My Neighbor* a matter of importance. The book stands at the confluence of political science, economics, sociology, history, and religion. When it was written most of these fields of study leaned heavily on the issues raised by city and industry. In the interval none of these disciplines has provided Canadians with a literature on the city, preferring the 'macro' concerns of province, region, and nation. Even in religion, while the Social Gospel escalated its concern to the social order – or even the international order – as a whole, others turned beyond the beyond to the 'wholly otherness of God.' Urban studies are only now beginning again with some force, and not only is *My Neighbor* an essential source in the background of that enterprise, but it remains one of our few accessible routes back to the era of the rise of the modern Canadian city and the first urban reform movement.

It was not quite correct of Woodsworth to observe in 1908 that only then were city problems beginning to require serious attention. As early as 1851 Toronto had discovered over three thousand children in her midst living with neither education nor familial restraint, and had promptly ended her opposition to free schools. Clerics in the late 1880s had become aware that poverty and the class structure of the city were impeding the propagation of the gospel and had begun innovations of which Woodsworth was the heir at All Peoples' Mission, Winnipeg. The struggles of labour and capital had become intense enough to require the appointment of a royal commission in 1886, civic corruption in Montreal had led a Montreal businessman, Herbert Brown Ames, to write a statistical analysis of social conditions in Montreal, *The City below the Hill* (1897), and to embark on a campaign of reform. Municipal ownership of the great civic franchises was already a warm issue in the 1890s, as was the remodelling of city government.

In the meantime, the less partisan but more sensational press, particularly the *Star* in Montreal, the *Telegram, World,* and *News* in Toronto, the *Journal* in Ottawa, the *News-Advertiser* in Vancouver, and the *Sun* in Winnipeg, had begun to provide a regular fare of urban conditions and reform which the more established papers were reluctant to indulge.[2] A substantial part of such news and commentary derived from the British and American scenes. The conditions of English cities as revealed in Henry Mayhew's *London Labour and the London Poor* (1851), William Booth's *In Darkest England and the Way Out* (1890), and Charles Booth's *Life and Labour in London* (1893), were familiar to many Canadians. Then (as now) the condition of the American city heightened the measure of concern Canadians gave to their own circumstances. The press religiously fed the public the latest and most lurid events in the travail of the American city – and not infrequently pointed a monarchist moral. Some undoubtedly knew Loring Brace's *The Dangerous Classes of New York and Twenty Years' Work among Them* (1880), and others the highly readable works of Jacob Riis, *How the Other Half Lives* (1890), *The Children of the Poor* (1892), and *A Ten Years War* (1900), and Lincoln Steffens, *The Shame of the Cities* (1904). Church editors, like W. H. Withrow of the

Canadian Methodist Magazine, kept substantial readerships abreast of the Protestant response to urban America with articles on city missions, institutional churches, deaconess orders and lay workers, and reviews of the works of Joseph Cook, Washington Gladden, Lyman Abbott, and other pioneer social gospellers.

There were probably few in the 1880s and 1890s who felt the shame of the Canadian city, but a growing company, including W. D. Le Sueur and W. A. Douglass and their Georgite Anti-Poverty Societies, pointed out that signs of an urban crisis in the making were not wanting. If problems were not as severe as in the larger American cities, that was no reason for complacency. Canadian cities had not reached the monstrous proportions of New York or Chicago, but the census of 1901 revealed that, while in the previous half-century the population of Ontario had doubled, Toronto had grown six times over; Quebec province had almost doubled in numbers, but Montreal almost five times. Especially in the 1880s many lesser centres had grown well in advance of the general population increase. By 1901 almost one out of every four Canadians was living in a town or city of five thousand or more.

After the turn of the century, concern intensified as Canadian Clubs, Empire Clubs, church groups, women's organizations, and associations of young men and young women, with increasing frequency secured lecturers on the subject of the city and its problems. The churches, the YMCAs and YWCAs, and the universities, after 1902, spread a network of city missions, social settlements, and institutional churches across the country and propagandized their constituencies for their support. Municipal governments sponsored magazines like *Municipal World* and the *Western Municipal News,* and other journals like the *Canadian Magazine* carried articles on urban reform with increasing frequency. In 1907 S. Morley Wickett edited for English Canadians a collection of such articles in *Municipal Government in Canada;* three years later French Canadians were offered a broad scheme of civic advance by G.-A. Nantel in *La Métropole de demain.* When the newly founded Canadian Political Science Association held its first conference in 1913, municipal government was the focus of attention. Participants were probably surprised to hear W. B. Munro of Harvard conclude that Canadian city government was based more on the American than the British model, with a system of separate boards, commissions, and officers all deriving equally from the sovereign electorate, frustrating unified administration and impeding reform. The growing urban middle class, however, was probably more concerned with problems of sanitation and food supplies than with theories of government and willingly supported campaigns such as that of Dr Charles Hastings, later Toronto's medical health officer, for pure milk in 1908. More impressive still were the occasional threats to civic peace and order, as when a Toronto streetcar strike exploded on 22 June 1902 into a violent confrontation of strikers and the militia. That, too, was a time to recall many events in American urban history — and to ponder deeply.

In the first years of this century the concern for urban affairs mounted, as it had in the early 1880s in the United States, in direct response to the phenomenal growth of urban populations in conjunction with an astonishing increase in, and a shift in the source of, immigration. Between 1901 and 1911 the urban population of the country increased 62.28 per cent. Whereas in 1901 there had been fifty-eight cities with a population of over 5,000, in 1911 there were ninety. Four cities, Montreal, Toronto, Winnipeg, and Vancouver, then numbered over 100,000; Montreal was approaching the half-million mark. More alarmingly, Toronto and Montreal very nearly doubled in the decade, Winnipeg multiplied four times over, and Vancouver nearly so, while newer prairie cities like Calgary and Regina grew by ten times and more.[3] Had the influx been of one language and nationality it would have placed intolerable burdens on civic development; but it was almost as varied in language and nationality as it was possible to imagine. While the Canadian government avidly promoted the flood of immigration, Canadians of all classes grew anxious over the social consequences. Serious social problems were obviously in the making when steamship companies scoured Europe eager only for the price per head; when minor potentates like a self-styled 'King of the Italian Workers' in Montreal arranged the arrival of hundreds of Italians with neither jobs nor resources; and when the occasional agency did a brisk business supplying strike-breakers for Canadian industries in the throes of labour disputes.

In spite of the number and diversity of immigrants between 1901 and 1911, the proportions of British and French in the population declined only three and two percentage points respectively in the decade.⁴ The statistical averages, however, hardly gave the full picture, since the immigrants were not evenly distributed. While two-thirds of Ontario's immigrants in the decade were British-born, the number of foreign-born was double that of British birth in Saskatchewan and Alberta; and whereas recent immigrants constituted only 20 per cent of Ontario's population in 1911, in the four western provinces they composed about 50 per cent.⁵ It was not more alarming statistics but the concentration of population that made the social problems of immigration so much worse in the cities.

In 1908 Woodsworth had written *Strangers within Our Gates,* an important early study of immigration. As that first book was being prepared for reprinting, the manuscript of *My Neighbor* was on its way to the publishers. It, like his first book, had in the first instance been conceived and requested by F. C. Stephenson as a textbook for his Young People's Forward Movement for Missions, and reflected the course Methodist young people's interest and study had recently been taking. Since Woodsworth not only derived his personal financial support from the movement but also found his largest original audience for his books through its agency, Stephenson and his Young People's Forward Movement merit more than passing mention. At the end of the century, when the missionary movement was reaching its height and North American churches had far more applicants than they could finance, Stephenson had met a blank wall in his efforts to join the ranks of overseas missionaries. Unwilling to accept refusal he had devised a simple but ingenious scheme of self-support by canvassing and pledging Methodist young people's groups (Epworth Leagues) in his region to finance him directly by means of a small monthly levy per member. The notion proved contagious and in 1894 Stephenson soon found himself at the centre of a development spreading through Methodist and other young people's organizations. It leapt the border into the United States in 1897, and Woodsworth himself carried the idea to Britain shortly after. So valuable had Stephenson's work become that, by 1904, now a fully trained and ordained medical missionary, he was persuaded to stay at home and become a full-time secretary to the whole enterprise in Canada.⁶

The scheme was much more than a mindless gathering of pennies and shipping of missionaries. Stephenson assiduously promoted intensive study in the organizations touched by it, and informative inter-communication between missionaries (home and foreign) and their group supporters. Young people's groups had already shown an interest in the Social Gospel, and Stephenson was concerned both to enhance their interest and deepen their knowledge. As much as any single person, he was responsible after 1904 for rearing, especially in the Methodist church, a generation of laymen prepared to walk a considerable distance with the Social Gospel. He early established summer schools to further the work, and was soon in the midst of a substantial publishing enterprise comprising a monthly bulletin of letters from missionaries, pages for several periodicals, and textbooks.

In 1901 a conference of church youth leaders in New York decided to project a series of Forward Mission study courses for the Canadian and American movements, each to focus on a textbook. By 1911 at least eighteen texts had been published, including *Aliens or Americans* (1906) by H. B. Grose and *The Challenge of the City* (1907) by Josiah Strong. However, there was no Canadian on the editorial committee, and the results were painfully obvious. Strong's book had precisely one sentence for Canadians: 'Canada must face the double problem of the city and her own great Northwest' (p. 265). A chart in the book erroneously suggested that Canada was more urban than the United States in 1891 and 1901.[7] Stephenson could hardly have been satisfied with the series. Despite pressure from his superiors on the Mission Board to use the American inter-denominational series where possible, he began and continued the publication of a separate series of Canadian texts for Canadians.[8] Woodsworth's books were texts 5 and 7 respectively in the Canadian series.

The circulation of any one of Stephenson's texts is difficult to calculate, but in 1911 he wrote that in the previous three years he had circulated over twenty thousand textbooks. Perhaps half of them were from his own series. It was curious that William Briggs, the church's publisher, never listed them in his advertisements, but Stephenson had his own captive market and, more as an educator than salesman, wrote, 'The fact that these are studied and discussed in YP [Young People's] meetings is much more important than that they are sold.'[9] The Epworth League and the other Canadian Methodist young people's groups at whom Stephenson chiefly

beamed his literature, alone had memberships totalling 62,085, with
an additional 18,395 in Junior Epworth Leagues.[10] Carefully worked
out programs stressed social subjects one week in each month. Given
sections of the prescribed text were assigned and related activities
suggested. Special series of articles to complement the text were
arranged in the *Epworth Era,* the *Missionary Outlook,* and the
Christian Guardian. Beyond the young people's groups, Women's
Missionary Societies and Men's Brotherhoods used Stephenson's
texts. Programs prepared for over 200,000 members of Methodist
Sunday Schools rehearsed some of the basic information the books
contained.[11] And for the use of all of these, Stephenson's
department prepared lantern slide lectures and resources for pictorial
displays, one of the results of which is the excellent photographic
collection on social problems of the period now in the United
Church Archives. One of Stephenson's books, C. B. Keenleyside's
God's Fellow Workers, became something of a runaway international
best seller in mission circles. There is no evidence that that happened
to either of the Woodsworth works, but with twenty-three summer
schools across the country in 1911 introduced to *My Neighbor,* and
the foregoing machinery geared to promoting its use, the book, and
even more the burden of its contents, must have had an impressive
circulation among Methodists alone.

The extent of the book's circulation outside the churches is a
matter of some speculation. Dr John MacLean, of another Winnipeg
city mission, who followed such matters, noted that it had met a
hearty response in the public press and on the platform.[14] Winnipeg
reviewers in the *Manitoba Free Press* and the *Telegram* greeted the
book warmly, noting its special value for 'the complex civic life

Whether other churches utilized the book is not clear. The
Presbyterians had also been moving more deeply into sociological
studies, and in 1911 published a textbook edited by W. R. McIntosh,
Social Service: A Book for Young Canadians, containing a chapter
on the city by O. D. Skelton. But neither they nor any other church
issued a work comparable to *My Neighbor.* A Maritime Presbyterian
reviewer urged it on all the churches, describing Woodsworth as 'a
citizen of every Canadian city and a contributing member of all the
churches.'[12] Dr A. P. McDiarmid, president of the Baptist Church's
Brandon College, agreed, finding it 'exceedingly suggestive and
stimulating, as well as broadly informative.'[13]

developing here,' and approved its central message of social solidarity. They appreciated its 'point and directness and practical force.' 'Ivanhoe' in the *Telegram* found no reason to criticize Woodsworth's subscription to gradualistic socialism, and 'The Bookman' in the *Free Press* added: 'It is a book to trust.'[15] Fellow social workers, J. H. T. Falk in Winnipeg and F. N. Stapleford in Toronto, were pleased at last to have a sociological work with Canadian content. The prominent Winnipeg reformer, F. J. Dixon, hoped it would shame Canadians into realizing that 'in the realm of progressive legislation this is one of the most backward countries.' One editor found it a useful medicine for those like C. H. Cahan who, incredibly, was urging Canadian Clubs to prepare to defend waterways and railways against a possible American invasion; reading *My Neighbor,* he prescribed, would make it clear that the real dangers to this country were ones common to both countries, and Boston and Montreal, Buffalo and Toronto, should be helping each other solve them. Only an American reviewer found fault with the extensive quoting of some British and many American authorities. From one standpoint this was a weakness in the work, but most Canadian reviewers were more than thankful to have so convenient a short course through the best literature on the subject of urban sociology. The book had other uses as well. The *Woman's International Quarterly* in London, England, prescribed it, along with Woodsworth's earlier study, as an antidote for highly coloured immigration advertisements. At the same time the journal expressed its sympathy for the civic agony of a young nation being invaded by contingents of forty-one nationalities.[16] The book evidently found its way to quite a diversity of reviewers and, if the reviewers are any guide, to a considerable and admiring general readership.

   It was not simply as a compilation of matters of fact and commentary, however, that the book made its mark, but by two apparently contrary characteristics: eclecticism and single-mindedness. Woodsworth readily confessed to the former, and undoubtedly his enthusiasm for most of the reform programs of the day broadened the range of his appeal. It was as easy to accept the book as an application of the parable of the Good Samaritan, from which the title was taken, as it was to hail it as an outline of the next steps towards a socialist commonwealth. There was, however, a guiding idea behind his eclecticism which accounts for the subdued

intensity which pervades the book. That was the idea of social
solidarity. Whatever Woodsworth touched he viewed in its light and,
despite his disclaimers of literary pretence, his style not infrequently
becomes genuinely eloquent as the subject matter moves closer to
this centre of his thought.[17]

The book was clearly of national importance, and many agreed
that Woodsworth was the man best prepared to write it. It could
hardly have been written by himself or anyone else much before
1911. Brandon, in which he grew up, and Winnipeg, which he
experienced as a student in the 1890s, were still, like most Canadian
cities, focused more upon their rural hinterlands than upon
themselves. He had experienced the problems of British and
European cities, and some of the responses to them, during his
studies and travels of 1899-1900; but the pertinence of the
experience was not yet apparent to him. Back in Canada he had been
happy with the consoling observation that the Canadian poor were
still honest and independent. In 1905, when an assistant minister
in a large Winnipeg church, he teamed up with Salem Bland of
Wesley College in a series of sermons on the city; but in 1907 he
could still write as though the countryside and its virtues provided
the final solution to the problem of the city.[18] What happened to the
Canadian city after 1901, and what happened to Woodsworth, thrust
in 1907 into the worst of Canadian civic problems as superintendent
of All Peoples' Mission, Winnipeg, changed all that.

Like the Fred Victor Mission in Toronto, All Peoples' had begun
some years before as a Sunday school class, the network of whose
little lives had slowly involved church workers in ever-widening
circles of social activity. By 1911 Woodsworth had created a
multifaceted institution with several bases in Winnipeg's north end.
Institutes, settlements, and neighbourhood houses provided religious
services in foreign languages; men's, women's, and children's
associations and clubs; language, industrial, and household science
classes; concerts; lectures; libraries; gymnasiums; baths; community
and hospital visiting; and relief. There were, of course, assistants: an
ordained man, eight deaconesses, three theological students, four
'kindergarteners,' a director of boys' work, two students training for
special work with language groups, two young women in training for
settlement work, and some hundred volunteers from Wesley College
and the city generally. The miracle was that any book, let alone two

pioneering studies, was written in the midst of such a development. But Woodsworth found time in these years to become one of the most widely read Canadians on social and civic subjects and, as well, to become the centre of efforts to rationalize city welfare agencies in Winnipeg, to serve on the civic playgrounds commission, and to act as the Ministerial Association's representative on the Trades and Labor Council. Through the last, he became labour's representative on the provincial Royal Commission on Technical Education during 1911-12. The years 1907-11 had been ones of total immersion in the city problem.

Woodsworth was not only engaged across a broad front of action, and reading widely, but, as a stream of articles in the secular and church press testify, he was almost constantly reflecting on the nature of the social problems before him. That was probably one reason why a reporter could note; 'He has no sense of humour – he really hasn't.' But another result was that he broke out of his agrarian bias to become both personally attached and committed to the city, and an authentic spokesman of urban reform.[19] He recognized what few other urban reformers realized, that, with continued mechanization, the growth of the modern city was becoming a self-sustaining phenomenon. The city was the future of civilization. Still more, he presented the clearest and most pointed articulation of the proposition that the fundamental inter-dependence of the city required total rather than piecemeal solutions. There was an implied collectivism in the proposals of most urban reformers – indeed of most reformers – of the time. That was an extension of the late nineteenth century's reharnessing of the state for social efficiency and the public good. But Woodsworth's social vision went beyond the agencies of the state and high-level civic planning and reorganization to embrace the development of a lively social consciousness and co-operative solutions by voluntary groups. The publication of *My Neighbor* marked as clearly as any event the arrival of a time for Canadians to engage in a large revaluing of their traditions. 'Our British ancestry, our Protestant traditions, our frontier training,' he was to write in 1913, 'have developed a sturdy independence, but have left us "short" on those elements which are essential to the co-operation involved in our complex modern life which finds its highest expression in the city.'[20] It was significant that whenever Woodsworth turned to rural problems after writing *My Neighbor,* his proposed solutions reflected the social values he saw implicit in the city.

Woodsworth's thoroughgoing social approach to the city was not simply compounded of observation, for he was, after all, his father's child, a son of a Methodist moralism that made it not difficult to see self-interest and economic greed in every influence corrupting the city. He was a member of a denomination with a long tradition of practical idealism and a doctrine of personal perfection in love in this life. Such elements from his past had been subjected to the transforming influence of the Social Gospel, rising about him in these formative years, and a testimony to whose influence upon him lies in the remarkable number of its works cited in his chapter references. His anticipation of a "new social revolution" was predicated upon a belief that "more and more the altruistic in aim is predominating in the efforts of men," and that social perfection was the proper goal of humanity.[21] The Social Gospel provided the hopeful context not only for his appreciation of urban problems and his solutions but also for his total conception of the city and its significance. With the writing of *My Neighbor,* Woodsworth himself became a major exponent of the Social Gospel. For him, faith was now supremely expressed in the spirit of social service and the city was not only its testing ground but, by the designs of a providential social evolution, the agency and the scene of its ultimate demonstration.

The city, however, was not to remain the centre of Woodsworth's career. He was to spend two more years at All Peoples' and in 1913, the year of his resignation, under commission from the Methodist and Presbyterian churches, he undertook social surveys of several Canadian cities along with Bryce Stewart and W. A. Riddell. Social welfare and research continued to preoccupy him, along with much travelling and speaking, until the middle of the war when the collision of his pacifism with wartime patriotism disrupted his life and drove him closer to the labour movement. Following the Winnipeg General Strike of 1919 his avowal of labour politics led him back to north Winnipeg, but now as a member of Parliament representing the people he had laboured for so earnestly at All Peoples'. The building of a national farmer-labour party, the task that occupied the rest of his life, was consummated in 1933 with the founding of the Co-operative Commonwealth Federation (CCF), the forerunner of the New Democratic party. He presided over its early growth as leader until in 1939 his pacifist convictions led him to part company with party policy. He died in 1942. Although urban conditions remained a central part of his concerns, his farmer-labour politics and federal position caused him later largely to by-pass the city as an arena of social action and concern. As in the life of the nation, the city suffered an eclipse in the life of J. S. Woodsworth.

Scattered through *My Neighbor* are half a hundred proposals comprising a broad program for urban advance. Many have been implemented; others, like state responsibility for the health and legal defence of its members, are still being worked out. Some reforms are now themselves in need of reforming. After half a century of bureaucratic civic development, spurred in part by reformers like Woodsworth, some may prefer a more individualistic ideal than his (though he was never a statist by temperament or intention and the social consciousness he believed necessary to the continuance of reform was advocated as a completion and not a denial of individual freedom).

The new urban reformers of the 1970's will find some of his proposals too simple and his faith too confident, but much remains to link them. Woodsworth's lack of dogmatism makes his work more approachable than it might otherwise have been. His concern for driveways, parks, civic centres, playgrounds, ultimate community ownership of land, universal and humane minimum standards of life, the socializing of education and medicine, the personalizing of social welfare, rapid transit, the extension of galleries and museums, and the cultural enfranchisement of the masses, all have a distinctly contemporary ring. He could urge, as present reformers do, the by-passing of established civic political organizations, and the mobilizing of people in the wards. He and the new reformers share a driving hope for the future of the city; and there are anticipations in his book of their fear that the city might instead become the citadel of an inhuman technology, a tangle of transportation systems with meaningless destinations, a morass of information without communication. He remains 'a citizen of all Canadian cities,' and whether Woodsworth's ideal city ever exists, the true urban reformer will live in no other.

NOTES

1 *Strangers within Our Gates* (Toronto, 1909), p. 255.
2 For this information, for incidental items below, and for many
   valuable perspectives, I am much in the debt of Paul Rutherford,
   Department of History, University of Toronto, who provided
   me with a copy of his paper presented to the Canadian Historical
   Association, 1971, 'To-morrow's Metropolis: The Urban Reform
   Movement in Canada, 1880-1920.'
3 See *Canada Year Book*, 1913, chap. 3, Tables 6-8, analysis,
   p. 57, based on towns and cities of over 5,000.
4 *Ibid.*, Table 15, p. 69.
5 *Ibid.*, Table 21, p. 79.
6 See United Church Archives, Stephenson Collection, 'Search
   Guide'; C. C. Love, *Frederick Clark Stephenson* (Toronto,
   1957); F. C. Stephenson, *The Young People's Forward Movement for Missions* (Toronto, 1900).
7 The percentages are too large even when the population of all
   Canadian towns and cities are included in the calculation.
   Woodsworth uncritically reproduced the chart (see below,
   p. 17). The rest of the chart and Woodsworth's own statistics
   seem generally reliable.
8 United Church Archives, Stephenson Collection, Minutes,
   General Board of Missions, 5 Oct. 1907, p. 389.
9 *Ibid.*, Stephenson to T. E. E. Shore, 26 June 1911.
10 *Canadian Epworth Era*, Sept. 1912, p. 214.
11 See the program lists and outlines published regularly in the
   Epworth Era and the *Missionary Outlook*.
12 Public Archives of Canada, J. S. Woodsworth Papers, scrapbooks
   (hereafter cited as Woodsworth scrapbooks), vol. 29, leaflet
   containing reviews.
13 *Missionary Outlook*, Jan. 1912, p. 11.
14 Woodsworth scrapbooks.
15 *Manitoba Free Press*, 11 Nov. 1911; *Telegram*, 17 Oct. 1911.
16 The foregoing reviews are found among undated cuttings in
   Woodsworth scrapbooks, vol. 29. Oddly enough, the wide-
   ranging *Review of Historical Publications Relating to Canada*
   reviewed neither Woodsworth book.

17 Many were quite moved by the book. 'It filled me up so,' wrote
    Dr C. T. Scott of Brantford, that 'I had to preach on the theme
    on Sunday' (*Missionary Outlook*, May 1912, p. 107). For
    additional comments on the book, see *Canadian Epworth Era*,
    Oct. 1911, pp. 224-5; *Christian Guardian*, 4 Oct. 1911, p. 14;
    18 Oct. 1911, p. 26; *Nurses Alumnae Journal*, Aug. 1912,
    pp. 13-14.
18 United Church Archives, Letters to C. B. Sissons, 28 Aug. 1907.
19 See especially the personal statement of his perceptions of urban
    life on pp. 11-12.
20 *Weekly Free Press and Prairie Farmer*, 11 July 1913.
21 Woodsworth scrapbooks; *North Ender* (Winnipeg), 23 March
    1911; also, 'Social Perfection,' *Christian Guardian*, 23 April
    1913.

My neighbor

J. S. WOODSWORTH

Contents

Preface

The large immigration to this country and the rapid growth of our cities are two of the most important developments in our Canadian national life. In *Strangers within Our Gates, or Coming Canadians* an effort was made to call attention to the importance of our immigration problems, and at the same time stimulate a sympathetic interest in the new arrivals who are making their homes in our midst. The present text-book attempts a similar end in relation to city life. The sub-titles give the scope and purpose of the book, and suggest its limitations. It is not designed to be a dispassionate study of the social phenomena of urban life. It is written confessedly from the viewpoint of the Social Worker. Emphasis is placed on crying social needs, and on more recent and, perhaps, less familiar lines of social effort. For instance, normal home life, the interests of the well-to-do business and professional classes, and the well-established church activities are barely mentioned, not because they are of minor importance, but because the slums of the cities and the struggles of 'the workers' and the social reforms are neglected, and on these attention should be concentrated.

Free and extensive use has been made of the many excellent books and other publication dealing with city conditions in the United States. Canadians are urged to study these, as we in Canada are now just entering upon a stage of development through which the people of the United States have been passing during the last generation. We can and ought to learn much from their experience.

Quotations are numerous. The author has not set out to 'write a book,' but rather to present a situation. Wherever possible he has tried to place the study-class 'next to' the authoritative source of information. Conditions in Winnipeg are cited most frequently because they are most familiar to the author. But they illustrate social phenomena more or less common to all our cities. Local variations and details will readily present themselves to every reader.

The list of references at the end of each chapter is limited largely to books that are easily accessible and of use to the general reader.

Among the many to whom thanks are due for help in the preparation of this work are Miss Agnes Allan, now headworker in the Deaconess Settlement of Fred Victor Mission, Toronto, and the Secretary of the Young People's Forward Movement.

With slight equipment, with limited time and many distractions, the author is very conscious of the roughness of his work. But perchance he may help blaze a trail that will serve the immediate need, and the very inadequacy of which will call forth the best efforts of scientific experts whose far-reaching schemes will then be supported by an awakened and intelligent public interest. Dreams? — Yes, but dreams sometimes come true, and visions are prophetic.

The Mission House,
464 Stella Ave.,
Winnipeg.
June 15th, 1911.

The city with the lid off

So that it was in fact the speculum or watch tower of Teufelsdrockh; wherefrom, sitting at ease, he might see the whole life circulation of that considerable city; the streets and lanes of which, with all their doing and driving (Thun and Trieben), were, for the most part, visible there.

'I look down into all that wasp-nest or beehive,' have we heard him say, 'and witness their wax-laying and honey-making and poison-brewing, and choking by sulphur. From the Palace Esplanade, where music plays while Serene Highness is pleased to eat his victuals, down to the low lane, where in her door-sill the aged widow, knitting for a thin livelihood, sits to feel the afternoon sun, I see it all: – That stifled hum of Midnight, when Traffic has lain down to rest; and the chariot wheels of Vanity, still rolling here and there through distant streets, are bearing her to Halls roofed-in and lighted to the due pitch for her; and only Vice and Misery, to prowl or to moan like nightbirds, are abroad; that hum, I say, like the stertorous, unquiet slumber of sick life, is heard in Heaven! Oh, under that hideous coverlet of vapors, and putrefactions and unimaginable gases, what a Fermenting-vat lies simmering and hid! The joyful and the sorrowful are there; men are dying there, men are being born; men are praying, – on the other side of a brick partition, men are cursing; and around them all is the vast, void Night. The proud Grandee still lingers in his perfumed saloons or reposes within damask curtains. Wretchedness cowers into truckle beds, or shivers hunger-stricken into its lair of straw; in obscure cellars, *Rouge-et-Noir* languidly emits its voice-of-destiny to haggard, hungry villains;

while Councillors of State sit plotting, and playing their high chess-game, whereof the pawns are Men. The Lover whispers his mistress that the coach is ready; and she, full of hope and fear, glides down, to fly with him over the borders; the Thief, still more silently, sets-to his picklocks and crowbars, or lurks in wait till the watchmen first snore in their boxes. Gay mansions, with supper-rooms and dancing-rooms, are full of light and music and high-swelling hearts; but, in the Condemned Cells, the pulse of life beats tremulous and faint, and bloodshot eyes look out through the darkness, which is around and within, for the light of a stern last morning. Six men are to be hanged on the morrow. Comes no hammering from the *Rabenstein*? Their gallows must even now be o'building. Upwards of five hundred thousand two-legged animals without feathers lie around us, in horizontal positions, their heads all in nightcaps, and full of the foolishest dreams. Riot cries aloud, and staggers and swaggers in his rank dens of shame; and the Mother, with streaming hair, kneels over her pallid, dying infant, whose cracked lips only her tears now moisten. All these heaped and huddled together, with nothing but a little carpentry and masonry between them; — crammed in like salted fish in their barrel; — or weltering, shall I say, like an Egyptian pitcher of tamed vipers, each struggling to get its *head above* the others; *such* work goes on under that smoke counterpane! But I, *mein Werther*, sit above it all; I am alone with the stars.'

Carlyle, Sartor Resartus

Chapter 1

The modern city

And at night along the dusky highway near and nearer drawn
Sees in heaven the light of London flaring like a dreary dawn;

And his spirit leaps within him to be gone before him then
Underneath the light he looks at, in among the throngs of men;

Men my brothers, men the workers, ever reaping something new:
That which they have done but earnest of the things that they
        shall do.

Locksley Hall

Is it well that while we range with Science, glorying in the Time,
City children soak and blacken soul and sense in city slime?

There among the glooming alleys Progress halts on palsied feet,
Crime and hunger cast our maidens by the thousand on the street;

There the Master scrimps his haggard seamstress of her daily bread,
There a single sordid attic holds the living and the dead;

There the smouldering fire of fever creeps across the rotted floor,
And the crowded couch of incest in the warrens of the poor.

Locksley Hall, Sixty Years After

IN THE INCIDENT which was the occasion of the parable of the
Good Samaritan, the lawyer desiring to justify himself said unto
Jesus, 'And who is my neighbor?' That question has been asked in
and by every age. In our own day, when the ends of the earth are
being drawn together, when ancient prejudices and hereditary
hatreds are being overcome, when international conferences and
parliaments of religion link together the peoples, when a peace
tribunal has made the federation of the world no longer chimerical,
and the brotherhood of man is becoming an ideal — in this our own
glorious day, we are being forced to ask ourselves anew, 'And who is
my neighbor?'

Nowhere does the question come with greater force than in the
latest and most complex product of civilization — the modern city.
On the wild, lonely road between Jerusalem and Jericho the
desperate plight of the stranger would arouse some sense of duty in
the most promotive modern man. But when at breakfast this same
modern man reads that, through the negligence of someone, ten
workmen were maimed for life or hurled into eternity — well, what
is that to him? He hardly pauses as he sips his coffee. His eye and his
attention pass to the next news item — the rise in the price of wheat
or the account of the great race. Even if he should own stock in the
corporation in whose factories the unfortunate workmen had been
employed, it would hardly occur to him that he was even remotely
responsible for their injury or death. The directors, the manager, the
foreman, factory inspectors — a hundred officials come between him
and the victims of the accident. Countless legal and moral questions
complicate the situation and confuse the moral sense. But the
groaning of these men has gone up to God. If through indifference
or selfishness we protest, 'Am I my brother's keeper?' there comes
the inexorable reply, 'The voice of thy brother's blood crieth unto
me from the ground.'

Someone is responsible! Every unjustly-treated man, every
defenceless woman, every neglected child has a neighbor somewhere.
Am I that neighbor?

Not only do we need to learn who our neighbor is, but also how
we can help him. Again reverting to the parable, the only thing for
the Good Samaritan to do was obviously to bind up the stranger's
wounds and place him under proper care. But how difficult it is to
minister adequately to the needs of the injured workmen of whom
we have spoken, or those of their companions who run similar risks.

They are part of a system as we are part of the same system. We as individuals cannot help them as individuals. The whole system must be reckoned with – possibly completely changed. We find ourselves, as the business men say, 'up against a big proposition.' Yet we must face the situation. We must learn to be neighborly not only in the wilderness, or in the comparatively simple life of a country community, but in the crowded city with its many and complicated interests. How? Well, to discover that is the purpose of our present study.

'The City' – what contrasted pictures are suggested! What varied emotions are aroused! To many who live in the country and only occasionally have the opportunity of an all too brief pleasure trip to the city, the word is full of charm. It means shopping and concerts and sight-seeing and all kinds of excitement. After the quiet, hum-drum existence of the farm, many a young man and woman sympathizes with the sentiment:

> Had I but plenty of money, money enough and to spare,
> The house for me, no doubt, were a house in the city-square;
> Ah, such a life, such a life, as one leads at the window there!
>   ...
> *Bang-whang-whang* goes the drum, *tootle-te-tootle* the fife.
> Oh, a day in the city-square, there is no such pleasure in life!
>
>   Browning

Such enthusiasm for city life is, however, that only of the visitor who views it from the window. The novel sights and sounds soon become familiar. The higher the buildings, the less sunshine; the bigger the crowds, the less fresh air. The 'drum's bang-whang-whang and the fife's tootle-te-tootle' begin to get on our nerves. We become weary in the unceasing rush, and feel utterly lonely in the crowded streets. There comes a wistful longing for the happy life of 'God's out-of-doors' with the perfume of the flowers and the singing of the birds. But our work now lies in the city and in the city we must stay. As we penetrate more deeply into its life, we discover evils of which we had hardly dreamed. Pitfalls abound on every side; dark crimes are being committed; dreadful tragedies are being enacted in real life. We get behind the scenes; we see the seamy side. We look beneath the glittering surface and shrink back from the hidden depths which the yawning darkness suggests.

Grinding competition makes the struggle for a mere existence an
almost hopeless effort:

Oh, God! that bread should be so dear,
And flesh and blood so cheap.

And yet –

Stitch! Stitch! Stitch!
In poverty, hunger and dirt.
                                                                    Hood

And the horror of it all grows upon us till the city becomes a
hateful thing, from which we would flee in despair – a monstrous
blot on the face of God's fair earth.

But escape from it we cannot. Great social tides carry us back
again, and as the years go by we come gradually to know the city.
We not only see its lights and its shadows, but we begin to
understand their relation, and they assume for us a new significance.
We begin to take our part in the life about us. We feel the throb of
the great heart that beats somewhere beneath it all. We are learning,
growing, deepening.

One day we are returning from a happy holiday at the old home
in the country. The train hurries us away from the fields and the
woods. Darkness comes on and we can no longer see the farmhouses.
Then come straggling lights – 'We must be getting near the city.'
'City next, all change,' shouts the conductor. There is a general
movement among the passengers. Wraps are donned and hand
baggage placed in readiness. We rattle over the switches; a yard
engine goes clanging past. Now the lighted streets begin to flash by.
We're nearly in – the street cars once more – just over there is my
office, and a mile beyond is home. And a new and almost
overpowering emotion wells up within me. In all this *I* have a part; I
am a part of it all – and the city has ceased to be merely attractive
or repellent – it belongs to me and I to it. I have become a
citizen.

One of the most striking characteristics of the city is the contrasts
which it presents. We cannot do better than quote (after Wilcox in
The American City) Walt Whitman:

After an absence, I am now again in New York City and Brooklyn on a few weeks' vacation. The splendor, picturesqueness and oceanic amplitude of these great cities, the unsurpassed situation, rivers and bay, sparkling sea tides, costly and lofty new buildings, façades of marble and iron, of original grandeur and elegance of design, with the masses of gay color, the preponderance of white and blue, the flags flying, the endless ships, the tumultuous streets, Broadway, the heavy, low, musical roar, hardly ever intermitted, even at night, the jobbers' houses, the rich shops, the wharves, the great Central Park and the Brooklyn Park of Hills, the assemblages of the citizens in their groups, conversation, trades, evening amusements, or along the by-quarters — these, I say, and the like of these, completely satisfy my sense of power, fulness, motion, etc., and give me, through such senses and appetites, and through my æsthetic conscience, a continued exaltation and absolute fulfilment. But sternly discarding, shutting our eyes to the glow and grandeur of the general superficial effect, coming down to what is of the only real importance — personalities — and examining minutely, we question, we ask, are there indeed *men* here worthy the name? Are there athletes? Are there perfect women to match the generous material luxuriance? Is there a prevailing atmosphere of beautiful manners? Are there crops of fine youths and majestic old persons? Are there arts worthy freedom and rich people? Is there a great moral and religious civilization — the only justification of a great material one? Confess that to severe eyes, using the moral microscope upon humanity, a sort of dry and flat Sahara appears, these cities crowded with petty grotesques, malformations, phantoms playing meaningless antics. Confess that everywhere in shop, street, church, theatre, bar-room, official chair, are pervading flippancy and vulgarity, low cunning, infidelity — everywhere the youth puny, impudent, foppish, prematurely ripe — everywhere an abnormal libidinousness, unhealthy forms, male, female, painted, padded, dyed, chignon'd, muddy complexions, bad blood, the capacity for good motherhood deceasing and deceased, shallow notions of beauty, with a range of manners or rather lack of manners (considering the advantages enjoy'd) probably the meanest to be seen in the world.

These contrasts, whether they are merely superficial or of the more serious character suggested by our quotation, are but manifestations of the complex life of the city. In a rural district each family lives its own life in a large degree independently of the rest of the world. But in the city, before you can get breakfast you must have secured the services of the milkman, the baker, the butcher, and a score of other tradesmen, who, in carrying on their business, are directly dependent upon the commission agents and wholesale dealers, upon express companies and transportation systems. These in turn reach out arms in every direction and touch the whole commercial life of the country. Let the street cars stop, for instance, or the electric power fail, and the whole business of the city is immediately 'tied up.' City life is like a spider's web – pull one thread and you pull every thread.

It is an immense and highly developed organism in which each minutest part has a distinct function. Borrowing the language of Paul: 'Those members of the body which seem to be more feeble are necessary; and those parts of the body which we think to be less honorable, upon these we bestow more abundant honor; and whether one member suffereth all the members suffer with it; or one member is honored all the members rejoice with it' (I Cor. 12: 23, 26).

This mutual dependence is what the French Communists called Solidarity. By slow degrees we are learning that 'the welfare of one is the concern of all.' Let me illustrate. I have remained on a street car as it passed from a slum district through the business section to a beautiful residential suburb. First the car was filled with a motley crowd of all nationalities. Opposite me sat a poor wreck of a man, clothes dirty and foul-smelling and probably filled with vermin and disease. He got off down town, and within a few blocks the character of the passengers had entirely changed. The car was now largely filled with ladies returning from their shopping expeditions. A fashionably dressed woman took her place opposite me in the very spot previously occupied by the man of the slums, from whom, had he been there, she would have shrunk in disgust and fear. In the city, for good or ill, we are members one of another.

Yes, and we are more or less responsible for the welfare or degradation of our fellow citizens. A lady hastens early in the morning to the bargain counter. She returns elated with her prize, which she boasts she has bought at *less than it cost*. Away across the city a poor girl is working early and late making button-holes for a few cents a dozen. She is 'run down,' but can't afford the holiday

The march of immigration, from *The Sphere*

the doctor advised. Within six months she will be in the Tubercular Hospital and within another six months in her grave. She has been forced to sell her work *at less than it cost.* Has the bargain-hunter no connection with that factory-girl? She does not know her personally, but has she no duty toward her? If she subscribes to the Charity Hospital is her conscience clear? That dollar that she 'saved' on her purchase – to whom does it really belong anyway? A host of similar questions confront us at every turn as we pass through the city streets.

Few realize how recent has been the development of what has been termed 'The Modern City.' The ancient cities were often small and represented a civilization entirely different from that of our own day. The cities of the far East, too, form a class by themselves and cannot be included in this study. But the cities of Europe and America and other countries directly influenced by Western civilization are essentially a product of modern social and economic movements. Fred C. Howe (in *The City, the Hope of Democracy*) puts it strongly:

The modern city marks a revolution – a revolution in industry, politics, society and life itself. Its coming has destroyed a rural society whose making has occupied mankind since the fall of Rome. It has erased many of our most laborious achievements and turned to scrap many of our established ideas. Man has entered on an urban age. He has become a communal being. The increasing pressure of population is fast filling up the waste places of the globe. This, of itself, forecasts the life of the future. And in consequence, the city will no longer be an incidental problem. It has already become the problem of society and the measure of our civilization.

The extent of this change is seen in the drift of population. Already four-fifths of the people of the United Kingdom dwell in cities. But one-fifth of Britain's teeming population, and a diminishing fifth, lives on the soil it cultivates. In the United States we are so accustomed to an immense unoccupied Western domain that the growth of our city population fails to impress us. In our thoughts America is still an agricultural nation, and the city but an incident of our growth. But an examination of the census returns destroys this illusion. In 1800 but four per cent. of our population dwelt within city walls. By 1830 the percentage had crept up to six and

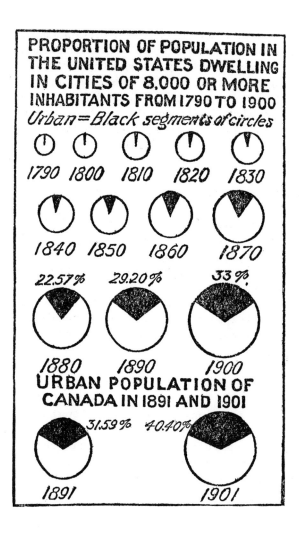

Growth of urban population in the United States and Canada

seven-tenths. Thirty years later, at the outbreak of the Civil War, five millions or sixteen and one-tenth of our people were urban dwellers. Since that time, the growth of industry, the expanding network of railways that has been woven across the face of the continent, the ever increasing inflow of immigration, have raised this ratio to thirty-three per cent. of the whole. To-day, more than twenty-five millions of America's population dwell in cities of over 8,000 inhabitants, while nearly forty per cent. of the total reside in communities of over 4,000 people.

Though Canada is so young a country it is being carried into the main current of modern social development. In the United States at the beginning of the last century out of a population of 5,308,483 only four per cent. lived in cities and towns of 8,000 and over. In Canada at the beginning of this century out of practically the same population (5,371,315) no less than forty per cent. lived in cities and towns of 8,000 and over.

Few of us have realized the rapid change that is taking place. We have thought of Canada as a series of agricultural communities; but within a few years half of our population will be living in cities and large towns. Quoting from the chapter on 'The City,' in *Strangers within Our Gates*:

Canada is leaving the country for the city. In 1891 thirty-two per cent. of our population was urban (cities of 10,000 and over); in 1901 thirty-eight per cent., a relative gain of six per cent. for the cities in ten years. The population of Ontario more than doubled from 1851 to 1901, but the population of Toronto increased over six times during the same period. The population of the Province of Quebec was almost twice as large in 1901 as in 1851, but that of Montreal was over four and one-half times as large. Manitoba is an agricultural Province, and yet one-quarter of the entire population is resident in the city of Winnipeg alone.

It will be of great interest to study the results of this year's census to learn whether with the great immigration to our Western prairies our urban tendencies have been at all retarded.

Probably we may accept the conclusion of Dr. Josiah Strong in *The Challenge of the City*: 'Thus in Europe, Asia and Africa we find

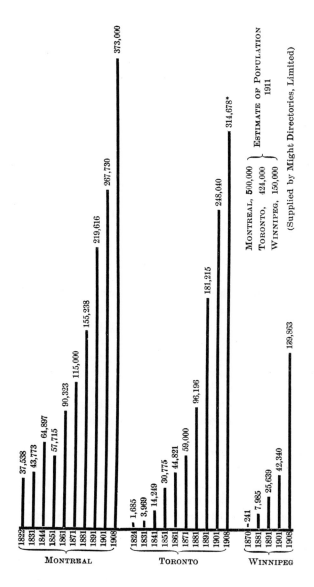

How our cities are growing   *Police census

that a redistribution of population is taking place, a movement from country to city. It is a world phenomenon. Some have imagined that it would prove temporary; that this flowing tide would soon ebb. But its causes are permanent and indicate that this movement will be permanent. This sudden expansion of the city marks a profound change in civilization, the result of which will grow more and more obvious.'

Many reasons have been advanced to account for this redistribution of population. Probably the most potent factor has been the discovery of the use of steam and modern mechanical inventions, with the various economic and social results which have followed in their train.

In England we can trace the development of the cities from the time machinery was substituted for hand labor. Prior to what has been termed the Industrial Revolution, goods were manufactured (made-by-hand) in every little village. When water-power could be utilized the village grew to a town. Where coal and iron were accessible the towns multiplied. But when machinery came into use a new era began; the city was born. Hand labor could not compete with the machine. Great factories arose and the village workers were driven to the factories. Then as processes became more complex, there came the division of labor. Ten men were required to make a single article, each doing his own particular part, and knowing how to do only that part. As this specialization went forward, the various departments of what had been a single industry became distinct, though closely-related, industries. Business attracted business and so the city grew, and so it will continue to grow. The use of electricity and the organization of industry and commerce have accelerated this centralization.

Following the stationary machine came the railway, through which distance has been almost annihilated. When men had to walk or use horses a village could be found every few miles, that is, within easy walking distance, and a market town within a few hours' drive. But now butter and eggs and vegetables are sent into the city every morning from farms scores or hundreds of miles away, and every outgoing train carries manufactured goods of all kinds to the most remote settlers. The modern city can draw on a continent for its supplies — yes, may even bring its fresh meat from the other side of the globe. On the other hand it may largely do the business of a province. For instance, witness the effect of departmental stores on country villages.

Further, machinery not only built up factories and gave quick transportation, but, applied to agriculture, reduced the number needed to produce the world's supplies. While food is necessary to life and while we must look largely to the farm for our food supplies and raw products generally, perhaps we have been apt to exaggerate the importance of the farm. The actual expenditure for food forms an ever lessening percentage of the family budget. Our 'wants' are multiplying in a hundred directions. We do not, cannot, live by bread alone. But even with regard to the 'necessities of life' the cost of preparation of products for consumption after they leave the farm is frequently far more than the original cost of production. A comparatively small number of farmers can supply the raw products required by a large population. As machinery is more largely used and farming becomes more scientific, a decreasingly small percentage of the population will be required on the farm.

Another important reason for the city's growth ought not to be overlooked. Men are learning how to live in the city. Formerly sanitary and moral conditions were so bad that the cities were not self-perpetuating, that is, their birth rate was less than their death rate. They maintained their existence or increased only by constant influx of healthy country blood. But conditions are rapidly changing, so that Dr. Adna F. Weber (in *The Growth of Cities in the Nineteenth Century*) states: 'The manner in which the modern growth of cities has taken place is rather a larger natural increase in the city populations themselves (lower death rate) than an increase in immigration from rural districts; the current of migration city-ward has been observed for several centuries, but it is only in the nineteenth century that any considerable number of cities have had a regular surplus of births over deaths.'

In view of these great tendencies which seem to be of a permanent character, is there any limit to the growth of cities? Dr. Strong sums up his argument: 'Because men are social beings, cities have always been as large as they could well be. But until the nineteenth century it was difficult to supply a large city with food, water and fuel. The lack of water resulted in extremely unsanitary conditions and a very high death rate. It also made the city an easy prey to fire, plague and pestilence. Famines occurred when grain was rotting on the ground only a few leagues away. The application of steam to transportation now makes it practicable to transport food from the other side of the world. Thus a tendency toward aggregation which has always existed has now been liberated, and the natural restriction to the growth of cities has been removed.'

But that there are other considerations which must enter into our calculations is pointed out by H. G. Wells in a book which is very suggestive, even if rather 'in the air' (*Anticipations of the Reaction of Mechanical and Scientific Progress upon Human Life and Thought*). Mr. Wells writes: 'But, indeed, these great cities are no permanent maelstroms. These new forces at present still so potently centripetal in their influence, bring with them, nevertheless, the distinct promise of a centrifugal application that may be finally equal to the complete reduction of all our present congestions. The limit of the pre-railway city was the limit of man and horse. But already that limit has been exceeded, and each day brings us nearer to the time when it will be thrust outward in every direction with an effect of enormous relief.'

The railway, the telephone, and similar inventions not only tend to bring the country into the city, but they carry the city into the country. So that we must, ultimately, according to Mr. Wells, look for the establishment of 'urban regions' in which the advantages of city and country will be combined.

Whatever the lines of future development, the importance of the city cannot well be overestimated. It is destined to exercise a dominating influence over the whole country. As Oliver Wendell Holmes says in *The Autocrat of the Breakfast Table,* 'The axis of the earth sticks out visibly through the centre of each and every town or city.' The cities are the ganglia or nerve centres of the whole of our social system. They are the very heart of our body politic. From the political, the social, the educational, the religious and the commercial standpoint, the city is the centre to which the whole nation is tributary, and which in turn moulds our national life. In *The American City,* Wilcox writes,

There are many reasons why the city problem is assuming national proportions. First, democracy, the tool with which we are cultivating human nature in America, has been badly damaged by its contact with city conditions. We must attend to our tool, repair it, and

perfect it, or find ourselves suddenly set back into political barbarism, doing hand labor only. Secondly, the city, as the centre of
civilization, and the distributing centre of the nation's intelligence,
tends to impose its ethical and social ideals upon the whole people,
irrespective of residence. Thirdly, as the accumulation of enormous
wealth in the hands of one man without a corresponding responsibility for its use with reference to social welfare is a positive menace
to the general well-being, so the concentration of wealth in a single city,
without a clear recognition on its part of its duty to the state,
becomes dangerous to the public weal.

Thus the city may become a menace to our whole civilization.
Again, let us listen to a warning voice from the Republic to the
south, 'The city has replaced simplicity, industrial freedom, and
equality of fortune with complexity, dependence, poverty and
misery, close besides a barbaric luxury like unto that of ancient
Rome. Vice, crime and disease have come in. The death rate has
increased, while infectious diseases and infant mortality ravage the
crowded quarters. The city has destroyed the home, and substituted
for it the hotel, flat, tenement, boarding-house, and cheap
lodging-house. Our politics have suffered and corruption has so allied
itself with our institutions that many despair of democracy. The city
exacts an awful price for the gain it has given us, a price that is being
paid in human life, suffering and the decay of virtue and the family.'
And yet, making full allowance for this which he calls the loss
account, Mr. Howe assures us that the city is the hope of
Democracy.

Despite current pessimism, the outlook for the American city is re-
assuring. The city contains the independent vote. Here are the militant
forces of our politics. As time goes on this independence will be extended to the state and the nation as well, with a consequent toning
up of the larger issues in American life. To the city we are to look for
a re-birth of democracy, a democracy that will possess the instincts
of the past, along with a belief in the powers of co-operative effort to
relieve the costs which city life entails. We already see this manifest
in many forms, in our schools, libraries, parks, playgrounds, kindergartens, bath-houses, where conservatism has not been so strengthened
by vested interests as to be able to resist democracy's coming.

As the city is moulding our social and political life, creating new institutions and developing a new spirit, may it not have a still wider effect on our thought and life? Surely in our laws, 'vested interests' and 'property rights' must give way before the rights of men and the welfare of society. And may we not expect that our religion will become less individualistic as we come to recognize that we must not only 'save our never dying soul,' but also 'serve the present age.'

These changed ideals of living will be reflected in our customs and also inevitably react upon our characters. The highly developed 'Social' man will be psychologically, ethically and spiritually far in advance of his ancestors, who had learned only to live to themselves.

What a vast field for study and speculation opens out before us, even as we take this hurried survey of the city. We might conclude our introductory chapter by two familiar quotations placed in unwonted juxtaposition.

And the Lord came down to see the city and the tower which the children of men builded. And the Lord said, Behold, they are one people and they have all one language; and this is what they begin to do; and now nothing will be withholden from them which they purpose to do.

Genesis II, verses 5 and 6

And I saw the holy city, new Jerusalem, coming down out of heaven from God, made ready as a bride adorned for her husband. And I heard a great voice out of the throne saying, Behold, the Tabernacle of God is with men and he shall dwell with them, and they shall be his peoples, and God himself shall be with them and be their God.

Rev. 21, verses 2 and 3

REFERENCES

'The Social Teaching of Jesus'
Shailer Mathews. New York: The Macmillan Co.
'Jesus Christ and the Social Question'
Francis G. Peabody. New York: The Macmillan Co.
'Christianity and the Social Crisis'
Walter Rauschenbusch. New York: The Macmillan Co.

'The Challenge of the City'
Josiah Strong. New York: Young People's Missionary Movement
'The Burden of the City'
Isabelle Horton. Fleming H. Revell Co.
'How the Other Half Lives'
Jacob A. Riis. New York: Young People's Missionary Movement
'The Growth of Cities in the Nineteenth Century'
Adna F. Weber. New York: Columbia University Studies
'The Coming City'
Richard T. Ely. New York: Thomas Y. Crowell
'Anticipations of the Reaction of Mechanical and Scientific Progress upon Human Life and Thought'
H. G. Wells. New York: Harper & Bros.

Chapter 2

The making of a city

Vast spaces of land for culture, exercise and garden round the cities, full of flowers, which, being everybody's property, none could gather; and of birds, which, being everybody's property, nobody could shoot.

John Ruskin

The housing problem, alike in town and country, is fraught with the most vital issues; a cheap, sanitary, spacious, stable fabric of a home, in wholesome, agreeable, and stimulating surroundings, is a prime necessary of wholesome family life. Such a home is impossible for the vast majority of the people under existing land tenures.

J. A. Hobson

WHEN we decide to make a home there are many things that must be considered. First of all, we determine the most suitable locality. Then, after the property is purchased, we decide where to build the house and proceed to lay out the grounds. Then comes the careful study of possible plans, with a veiw to having as many conveniences and as much comfort as possible. Last of all come the actual building operations.

But while it is often possible for an individual thus to map out his own course of action in building a house for himself, it is rarely that a city population thus deliberately plans its home — the City. Cities as a rule have grown up in a helter-skelter fashion — each man has considered only his own immediate needs, his particular operations being limited or modified only as they run foul of someone else's. Then the very medley of it all has made imperative some kind of order, with mutual concessions for the common good. But it is only in recent years that we are beginning to learn that as the city is not a mere aggregation of independent individuals, but rather a certain type of social organism, so the physical city must be considered as a whole and the various parts must be subordinated to the whole — yes, that their highest welfare is dependent on that of the whole.

With this sense of the unity of the city has come the forward look. We think not merely of to-day or to-morrow, but remember that we are only laying the foundations upon which, one day, will be built the greater city of the future.

Occasionally the location of cities is deliberately determined. For instance, Ottawa was only By-Town till it was decided that it should become the capital of Canada. But usually the undirected play of social forces has led to the establishment of our great cities.

In troubled times a strong fortress was often the nucleus of a large city. There men could live and trade in safety. Natural advantages there must be, and so in earlier times cities were found on the coast where there were good harbors, or along the rivers which were the regular avenues of trade, or at intersecting points on the great roads of travel. With the development of our railroad systems other factors have had a determining influence. It is curious that the great economic forces that are building up our modern cities are often vastly different from those that originally led to the establishment of these self-same cities. For instance, Fort Garry (the future Winnipeg) was placed at the junction of the Red and the

Winnipeg, old and new

Assiniboine, in order that it might capture the fur trade of the Indians, who paddled down these streams in their birch canoes. Little did these fur traders of a century ago think that they were selecting a site for one of the world's grain markets. Or later, nothing could have been further from the minds of the half-breed 'freighters' than that they were laying out the great thoroughfares of a cosmopolitan city. Yet the winding trails made by their 'screaking' Red River carts as they followed the broader curves of the Red and the Assiniboine have become Main Street and Portage Avenue.

It is true of the city, as of most things in this world, that the situation is generally not of our own choosing. Our part is to make the best of it.

Too great emphasis cannot be laid upon the necessity for a comprehensive city plan. Civic reforms of all kinds are dependent upon better living conditions and these in their turn are largely dependent upon the 'lay-out' of the city. Crime, immorality, disease and misery vary almost directly as the size of the lot, the breadth of the street and the number of parks. Even with the older cities much is being done in the way of city planning. In London, England, great thoroughfares are being run through crowded districts, parks are being opened up in the slums, unsightly waterfronts are being transformed; the 'old town' is hardly recognizable. These improvements have involved many millions of pounds and have been retarded by countless legal obstacles and sentimental prejudices, yet they are being pushed steadily forward with growing confidence.

In Germany city planning has come to be a distinct science. Just as we have architects and landscape gardeners, so they have experts who advise not only as to details, but who, so to speak, take a city in hand and make it over with a view to its future development. On this continent the cities are beginning to wake up, and we now have conferences on city planning. We always seem to begin with a conference – and sometimes end there. So within recent years we have had a plan for 'The Greater Chicago,' 'A City-Planning Exhibition' in New York, 'A Boston 1915 Movement,' and similar movements right across the continent.

In Canada we are beginning to build with an eye to the future, although as yet our cities have done comparatively little toward adopting comprehensive plans. But an interest is being gradually aroused and some movement of this character is under way in all our larger cities. Montreal furnishes a good illustration of the needs and the possibilities of city planning. At the first convention of the City Improvement League of Montreal (1910) Prof. Nobbs and Mr. W. S. Maxwell dealt with this question. The following extracts from the report of their addresses will bring before us the scope of what will doubtless be one of the most important of our public questions. Prof. Nobbs' argument is thus summarized:

1 By means of by-laws and regulations it is possible with foresight to regulate the kinds of building to be allowed in different districts.

2 Main thoroughfares should never be arbitrarily set out, except on level sites. It is impossible to say what it costs Montreal, in wear and tear of streets, tires and horse-flesh, to rise from the low to the high level by a gridiron plan so set that every slope is as steep as possible. Sooner or later we shall have to open up some great diagonals which will enable the slope to be taken at a trot.

3 The smaller streets should, in our climate, run north and south as far as may be, so that the majority of windows may get sun for part of the day. With our shading Mount Royal to the northwest and the lesser streets set northwest to southeast, an unfair division of light has been made.

4 Great avenues need seldom run straight for more than two miles and need to be closed by great monuments. This principle was illustrated by great examples in Berlin, Florence and St. Petersburg. We have some notable masses in our great churches, but the streets and churches have not been planned together and the effect of the architecture is largely wasted, e.g., there is only one worthy view of the dome of St. James, that is from Price Avenue down Mactavish Street.

5 Streets should be laid out for the handling of traffic; therefore two main streets should not intersect without considerable open space, nor should several busy streets converge in a small circus. These mistakes are costing London and Paris dear, while Berlin and Vienna have profited by the object-lessons.

6 In some modern city-planning, symmetry is carried to excess and becomes ineffective (except from a balloon or on paper) and wasteful, as at Washington and Columbia University – contrasted with ancient Rome or 18th century Nancy. Some of the finest city places are non-symmetrical, where great buildings and the intersection of some thoroughfare give occasion for expressing the

dignity of city life, based on common interests, rights, hope and
pride. Such are many Italian piazzas. If symmetry comes naturally,
let us by all means use that easiest of effects. But when the elements
bear the natural character of crookedness let us with great care plan
crookedly.

Mr. Maxwell said:

The Association of Architects holds to the belief that no city can
develop normally without a plan which determines its growth along
economic, hygienic and æsthetic lines – covering a period of at least
50 or 75 years. We may ask in what way Montreal has suffered
through the lack of an authoritative plan.

This question is easily answered without going into great detail.
First of all, it was a great blunder to construct the streets on this
side of the mountain at right angles to the hill, because of the
excessive grades, which in places exceed twelve per cent.; another is
the absence of communication from east to west in this part of the
city. This can now be remedied by running a street through valuable
property and demolishing some fine residences recently built! This
district is a splendid illustration of the folly of placing streets regardless of any coherent plan. Another hillside blunder was perpetrated
when the city neglected to provide by homologation for several
streets leading diagonally from the Craig Street level to that of
Dorchester Street. This brings us to another very important matter,
that of diagonal thoroughfares from one busy centre to another. We
have shown certain ones on our city plan, but realize that many
others will shortly be needed. Another instance of our want of
foresight is the lack of sufficient playgrounds and breathing spaces
for our citizens, and more particularly for the young ones, who are
unable for various reasons to go to our existing, and, in many cases,
distant playgrounds. Parks, gardens, commons, public squares are the
lungs of a city. If Montreal were more generously provided with
playgrounds, especially in the congested districts, juvenile crime and
the mortality from tuberculosis and other ailments would be
materially decreased. The question may be asked, Why playgrounds
instead of squares with diagonal paths and the usual cast-iron
fountain surrounded by 'keep off the grass' signs? This is easy to
answer, because in crowded residential districts a playground is more
valuable than a park, on the theory that the health and morals of the

people are of more importance than the precarious existence of a
few blades of grass. As a further justification of playgrounds I quote
Judge Lindsay of Denver, who says that nine-tenths of juvenile
crimes can be attributed to the fact that the activities of the child
have no legitimate outlet.

Having stated a few of the things we lack, it is high time to
examine some of our precious possessions. Our river is superb,
and our harbor is fast becoming one of the most modern in the
world, which may be construed as a tribute to the Board of Control
system by a limited number of intelligent and qualified men. We
have not devoted much of our time to the harbor front, but have
studied very carefully the waterfront to the west of the Victoria
Bridge. Here we have a superb chance to carry a driveway along the
dike, with parks and playgrounds at intervals. This is the reasonable
thing to do, because this part of the river front is not suitable for
docks owing to the shallowness of the river; because the view to be
obtained therefrom is beautiful, and because, as this land is owned
by the city, the scheme can be realized at the cost of development
only. Our most precious possession is Mount Royal Park. This is a
tribute to the principle we advocate of having an official plan determining the line of future improvements, because this park was
conceived on a scale which considered the future. It was laid out by
Frederick Law Olmsted, one of the great masters of park planting,
and to this day we insist that nothing shall be done which will
violate the conception he formulated. Now, what are we doing for
the future? Our city grows as it never grew before; districts which
were open country a few years ago are crowded with two and three
story flats. Is this intelligent city building? Is it an economic policy?
Certainly not; we shall pay four-fold for our indifference in the near
future.

Here are some of Montreal's difficulties and possibilities – what
about those of our own city?

As our cities are so largely dependent upon the railways, a city
plan must provide for rapid and economic transportation of both
people and goods. Frequently competing companies obtain an
entrance to the city and locate their passenger stations and freight
sheds without any regard to the convenience of the public. Thus
railways have spoiled residential districts, rendered streets dangerous

or valueless, and made the transfer of passengers and freight both awkward and expensive. The city itself ought to retain absolute authority over terminal facilities, whether of the railroad or the water-front, if there be such. The railroads owe their traffic and their profits to the city and their selfish interests ought to be entirely subordinated to the public welfare.

The distance one may live from his work depends almost entirely upon the time consumed in getting to and from it. Distance is best measured by time. A man can afford to live at least thirty minutes from his work — perhaps an hour; if he walks, that means, say, two miles; if he drives, five miles; if he uses the street car, five miles, the suburban trolley, ten miles, the express, thirty miles. Multiply transportation facilities and every citizen may own his own suburban home — yes, and do his work in a district that resembles a park rather than a jungle. Here lies the necessity for the city either owning or absolutely controlling the street car and suburban systems, so that the lines may be extended as the needs demand, and the service and rates made adequate and reasonable.

Another matter of primary importance is the adequate provision for streets and lanes. These are essential not only for light and air, but for communication of every kind. Frequently the greed of real estate investors has given us narrow streets and short streets and half streets and no lanes, and then the greed of the street car and gas companies has appropriated what little we have, and what ought to belong to everybody belongs to nobody.

One principle ought to be clearly understood and never forgotten, *the city owns its streets*. Street railways, electric light and gas companies, telephone and telegraph companies have absolutely no right to the public streets, and should be given privileges only under conditions that are in the interest of the public, and can be readily enforced. What an amount of inconvenience and loss, of friction and litigation this would save!

Two practical points ought to be noted. Looking to the future, before any new subdivision is placed upon the market the city should insist that the most adequate provision be made for streets and lanes — yes, and for good-sized lots and parks and playgrounds.

And when it is necessary to undo the bungling of an earlier generation and open new wide streets through congested districts, this may generally be done without entailing serious expense to the public. The course often taken on this continent is for the city to buy up at enhanced prices the land necessary for the proposed improvements, and then to pay heavy compensation for supposed depreciation in adjacent properties. In England and elsewhere, they have learned the use of what is known as excess condemnation. The city expropriates the property along the line of the proposed streets. When the improvements are made the value of this land is greatly increased, and the city can sell at a profit sufficient often to cover the entire expenditure involved. It is said that in Rio Janeiro a space two-and-a-half miles long and three hundred feet wide was expropriated through the settled city from water to water, for a boulevard one hundred feet wide. The sale of the one hundred feet on each side of the boulevard paid within eighteen months for the whole improvement. Why not, it may be asked, apply this principle even more widely, and let the city rather than the private speculator reap the benefit of the increased value of lands in or adjacent to the city?

Much might be said about the need of beautifying the streets, of insisting that residences on a street conform to a certain type of architecture and be set back from the street at a somewhat uniform distance, that the height of business blocks be regulated, and that they be confined to certain districts. Quoting again from the address of Prof. Nobbs,

The streets! The telegraph, telephone and light and power poles make our main thoroughfares look like a Chinese harbor after a typhoon! The lamp-posts, if posts they may be called!!! The straggling maples on the street — trees so beautiful in a wood, so sad and sickly in a city avenue — and elms and poplars grow so well in this town! The water-tanks, the sky-signs, the horrible advertisements painted in epic scale on the flanks of buildings, the lettering falling like a veil over many a fair piece of architecture, and the hoardings bedight with play-bills; all these things are without decency and contrary to the expression of any civic spirit of virtue; they might all be ameliorated without cost.

Truly most of our city streets fall far short of the standards of the City Beautiful.

In our city planning we must reserve abundant open spaces for parks and playgrounds. Land is valuable for residential and commercial purposes. But houses and stores are worse than useless unless the health and morals of the people are conserved. Mr. J. J. Kelso of Toronto makes a strong appeal for Playgrounds:

We have been going distinctly backward during the past few years. We are gradually losing the old familiar playgrounds, and the athletic clubs that we had a few years ago have passed out of existence. Those of you who were once Toronto boys will remember the Queen's Park. Children used to spend many happy hours along the side of the little stream that ran through there, and around the pond where the swans and other birds were to be found. In those days there were ample playgrounds in which all the children of Toronto could enjoy themselves, but they have almost entirely disappeared, and if you go to Queen's Park now you will read the ominous sign, 'Ball playing strictly prohibited,' and the other day an order was issued prohibiting coasting down the hills.

This subject of playgrounds and play life has been lost sight of in the civic life of Toronto. There is no reason why we should not have numerous playgrounds. If I had my way I would take the block of land in front of the City Hall and establish there a playground and open-air gymnasium, and have one of the best athletic instructors directing the sports of the young people. Just consider for a moment the influence that would have on the social life of the people of Toronto! You would have an object-lesson always before the people, of rational enjoyment; and the happiness of the children playing there would reflect into the lives of men and women passing by, who need something to cheer them up. Nowadays we are getting to look on the sad side of life altogether too much, and we ought to keep constantly in mind that man needs diversion, needs to forget the cares and worries of business life, and if we cannot be happy ourselves, if we are too busy making money to take time to enjoy life, let us at least provide the facilities for boys and girls to be young while they are young.

In every city small playgrounds for the little children ought to be found within every few blocks, and athletic grounds for the young people within easy reach. Then, scattered through the city, and surrounding it, should be a series of smaller and larger parks, that

The problem of the children

A supervised playground, Toronto
Children asking for a playground

would enable every tired mother to wheel her baby out for an hour in the afternoon and the whole family to have a weekly half-holiday on the grass under the trees. Is this asking too much?

Our city plan would be very incomplete indeed — as most of our cities really are — if it lacked a 'civic centre.' This should be dignified and beautiful, the pride of the citizens, the very embodiment of the highest civic ideals. We think of some of the old-land cities with their great central squares around which are grouped the city hall, the museum and library, and from which a wide boulevard opens up a magnificent view of the old cathedral. In this country a departmental store gains possession of the principal corner. The city hall is squeezed into a narrow street, the library is built in an out-of-the-way place, and the historic old church, being on valuable land, is pulled down to provide a site for a magnificent bank! Now is the time, while our cities are young and land comparatively cheap, to make the most liberal provision for the needs of the future.

Other matters of vital importance are the making provision for an adequate supply of pure water and facilities for disposing of sewage. Our city, in addition to being well laid out, must be in every respect a healthful place in which to live.

This leads to the need of building regulations. The city owns its own streets. It ought to control every square foot of property within its limits. Property rights have been so drilled into us that there are some who say that a man has a right to do what he likes on his own land. But ultimately all land belongs to the state or the community. Feudal tenure has long since passed, but the very fact that taxes have always been levied without the principle being questioned is sufficient proof that the individual holds his property only conditionally. In practice there is a growing tendency to impose upon the individual regulations that make for the common good. Land may be expropriated for public purposes. A man may not carry on, even on his own premises, what may be a public nuisance. He must, through taxes, join in great communal undertakings, such as the installation of a water-works system; this really under threat of forfeiture, for in default of payment of taxes his property would be sold. In the cities, where men must live in close proximity, these regulations are increased and carried out to the smallest detail. If a man erects a house he must, within specified areas, build of certain material (i.e., for fire protection), put in a certain style of plumbing (i.e., for health protection), and, after his house is built, permit only so many people to occupy any room in it. Such restrictions are absolutely essential. The lack of them has, in older cities, led to hardship, disease, immorality and crime of every description. Only after a long, hard fight are 'vested interests,' which phrase often means 'private greed,' being forced to give way. But the city is awakening to a consciousness of its powers, and learning how to use them for the general welfare of its citizens.

Lawrence Veiller in a book entitled *Housing Reform,* recently published by the Russell Sage Foundation, writes:

Every American city has its housing problem. While in no two cities the same, in all there are certain underlying conditions which find common expression. Bad housing conditions generally first manifest themselves when several families are found living in a dwelling intended originally for a single family. Then, with the increase in population, there comes the building of regular tenement houses, usually before any restrictions have been thought of by the community. Rapidly from this point develop the evils of cellar dwellings, unsanitary privies, lack of drainage, inadequate water supply, filthy out-premises, defective plumbing, dark rooms and halls, overcrowding, the taking in of lodgers, congestion, excessive rents, the sweating evil and those other manifestations of modern social life which are too often seen in our large cities.

The causes of these evils are not to be found in any one thing, but are to be traced through a variety of influences operating through considerable periods of time. Some of the evils are peculiar to a single community, but most of them, sooner or later, are found in all cities. The chief underlying factor which stands out in every community is that they are, in nearly every case, due to neglect and ignorance. Neglect on the part of the community, failure of its citizens to recognize evil tendencies as they develop; dangerous ignorance on the part of citizens and public officials of what is going on within the city's gates; a feeling of safety and of confidence that all must be right because they see little that is wrong, that things cannot be bad as long as they are hidden; a false civic pride which believes that everything in one's own city is the best, a dangerous sort of apathy content to leave things as they are, a *laissez faire* policy which brings forth fruit of unrighteousness.

Invariably accompanying these two causes, but to a lesser degree, is found a third, greed. Greed on the part of those persons who, for the sake of a larger profit on their investments, are willing to traffic in human lives, to sacrifice the health and welfare of countless thousands.

We cannot do better than append Mr. Veiller's 'Chapter of Don'ts':

Don't let your city become a city of tenements; keep it a city of homes.
Don't imagine that there is no necessity for action because conditions in your city are not as bad as they are elsewhere.
Don't build a model tenement until you have secured a model housing law.
Don't attempt to legislate first and investigate afterwards.
Don't permit any new houses to be built that do not have adequate light and ventilation and proper sanitation.
Don't legislate merely for the present.
Don't permit the growth of new slums; prevention is better than cure.
Don't urge that all new houses shall be fireproof.
Don't permit the occupancy of new houses if built in violation of law.
Don't lightly give discretionary powers to the officials who enforce your housing laws.
Don't urge the creation of a Tenement House Department unless you have more than 25,000 tenement houses.
Don't complain of the enforcing authorities until you are familiar with their methods of administration.
Don't tolerate cellar dwellings.
Don't let the poor be denied a liberal supply of water in their homes.
Don't permit houses unfit for human habitation to be occupied.
Don't urge at first the reconstruction of the older houses; let this wait until after other things have been done.
Don't permit privies to exist in any city; compel their removal.
Don't urge the destruction of unsanitary buildings; keep them empty if they are not fit for human habitation.

Don't tolerate the lodger evil! Nip it in the bud.

Don't take up minor matters, but attack the worst evils first.

Don't allow the enforcement of housing laws to be nullified by politicians.

Don't neglect the landlord's side of the question.

Don't repeat the talk about the poor not wanting good housing accommodation.

Don't urge the municipal ownership and operation of tenement houses.

Don't ask the poor questions about themselves in housing investigations, but about their houses.

Don't resort to criticism of public officials until you have tried co-operation.

Don't rely on the death-rate alone as an index of good or bad housing conditions.

Don't confuse the fields of public and private effort.

Don't cease your efforts when you have passed a good law; eternal vigilance is not only the price of liberty but of all progress.

REFERENCES

City planning and housing
'The Improvement of Towns and Cities and Modern Civic Art'
Charles Mulford Robinson. New York: G. P. Putnam & Sons
'Garden Cities of To-morrow'
Ebenezer Howard. London: Swan, Sonnensehein & Co., Ltd.
'The Improvement of the Dwellings and Surroundings of the People; the Example of Germany'
T. C. Horsfall. Manchester University Press
'Housing Reform'
Lawrence Veiller. New York: Charities Publication Committee
Reports of Commissions and Conferences on City Planning

Municipal control of public utilities
'The City, the Hope of Democracy'
Frederick C. Howe. New York: Charles Scribner's Sons
'The American City; A Problem in Democracy'
Delos F. Wilcox. New York: The Macmillan Co.

'Municipal Ownership in Great Britain'
Hugo R. Meyer. New York: The Macmillan Co.
'The Common Sense of Municipal Trading'
G. Bernard Shaw. London: A. C. Fifield

Chapter 3

The struggling masses

The People are the city.

Shakespeare

We have much studied and much perfected of late the great civilized invention of the division of labor; only we give it a false name. It is not, truly speaking, the labor that is divided, but the men — divided into mere segments of men, broken into small fragments and crumbs of life. The great cry that rises from all our manufacturing cities, louder than their furnace blast, is all in very deed for this — that we manufacture everything there except men; we blanch cotton, we strengthen steel, we refine sugar, we shape pottery; but to brighten, to strengthen, to refine, or to form a single living spirit, never enters into our estimate of advantages.

John Ruskin

The worst of the distressing poverty, as well as the irresponsible wealth, is traceable to economic institutions, to franchise privileges and unwise taxation; to laws which are open to correction as they were to creation. Conditions in the tenement are not ethical, not personal; they are traceable to the laws of our own enactment.

Howe

IN CANADA to-day we are all anxious for our cities to grow and our industries to increase. But few of us know the problems which large cities bring, or realize the dangers in modern industrial development.

The writer remembers clearly his first contact with social conditions in the cities of the old land some eleven years ago. Beautiful squares, historic palaces, old cathedrals, wonderful art galleries, the unaffected dignity, the inbred sense of honor, the ripe scholarship, the age-long culture – all these cast a potent spell, but even these could not blind him to the monotony and wretchedness of the lives of great masses of the people. The flowers of civilization were beautiful, but what of the millions of toilers submerged in the muck? They were struggling for an existence, at best degraded and miserable.

After all, it was good to get back to Canada. Many things might be primitive and undeveloped, but in contrast with the dwellers of the slums our poorest people seemed so clean and honest and independent. Above all there was a general friendliness and hopefulness that warmed one's heart.

A decade only has passed, but what changes! The whole social atmosphere is different. We can now read and hear sentiments like this,

The wage of the average worker on the whole has, during the past year, been enough to keep him and no more. His economic position is in no way improved. As a matter of fact, it is probably worse, since at no time of which we know has the working class received a smaller proportion of the goods it produced than right now. Moreover, the outlook is none too bright. If our prognostications be correct, the wheels of industry will run but slowly this winter, so that even the doubtful privilege of producing wealth for others will be denied many of them, and then where will we be? *Western Clarion*

It is easy to say that this 'growser' has been imported, but the significant fact is that conditions are such that this kind of talk expresses the mind of an increasingly large number of our city workers. It cannot be too strongly emphasized that almost unconsciously we have in Canada entered upon a completely new era.

A few years ago Upton Sinclair dedicated to the working-men of America a most revolting book, *The Jungle.* Of course it may have been over-drawn and highly colored and all that kind of thing, but it called attention to most serious evils existing in Chicago. But the writer has been surprised and startled to find how much of it he understands from personal knowledge of conditions in our own Canadian cities. Already we have in rudimentary form nearly all the evils that have cursed older nations. Surely we should study with the greatest care the economic and social forces that, having created our cities, are determining their destiny.

'You Canadians have,' said a London social worker, 'the grandest chance given to man – the youth of a new nation, with the inheritance and experience of an older one.'

If only our eyes can be opened in time, and if only we have the good sense to learn from the experience of others!

Hunter in his book on *Poverty* writes:

There are great districts of people who are up before dawn, who wash, dress and eat breakfast, kiss wives and children and hurry away to work or to seek work. The world rests upon their shoulders; it moves by their muscle; everything would stop if, for any reason, they should decide not to go into the fields and factories and mines. But the world is so organized that they gain enough to live upon only when they work; should they cease, they are in destitution and hunger. The more fortunate of the laborers are but a few weeks from actual distress when the machines are stopped. Upon the unskilled masses want is continually pressing. As soon as employment ceases, suffering stares them in the face; they are the actual producers of wealth who have no home nor any bit of soil which they may call their own. They are the millions who possess no tools, and can only work by permission of another. In the main they live miserably, they know not why. They work sore yet gain nothing. They know the meaning of hunger and the dread of want. They love their wives and children. They try to retain their self-respect, they have some ambition, they give to neighbors in need, yet they are themselves children of poverty.

In another place Hunter makes the following startling statement:

It seems reasonable to assume that the wages of the unskilled laborers in this country rarely rise above the poverty line. A certain

percentage are doubtless able to maintain a state of physical efficiency while they have work, but when unemployment comes and
their wages cease, a great mass of the unskilled workers find themselves almost immediately in poverty, if not indeed in actual distress.
It is safe to say that a large number of workers, the mass of unskilled
and some skilled workmen with their families, fall beneath the
poverty line at least three times during their lives — during childhood, in the prime of life (when young families are dependent upon
them), and at old age (when the children have married and left home
and the parents are past work).

Such are the appalling conditions in the United States. In England
things are worse. Mr. Charles Booth's researches showed that in
London about 30 per cent. of the entire population were unable to
obtain the necessaries for a sound livelihood. Mr. A. Scott Matheson
says: 'The deplorable truth is that honesty, sobriety and willingness
to work do not suffice to save thousands of worthy people from the
harsh clutches of permanent pauperism.'

In our own young country conditions are not so bad. Pray God
they never may be! But the same economic laws are at work as in
other countries, and unless checkmated will inevitably produce
similar results. Where lies the trouble? What is the real excuse of this
widespread poverty and its attendant evils?

Rauschenbusch in his admirable work, *Christianity and the Social
Crisis,* traces the effects of the introduction of the power machine:

The machine was too expensive to be set up in the old home workshops, and owned by every master. If the guilds had been wise
enough to purchase and operate machinery in common, they might
have effected a co-operative organization of industry in which all
could have shared the increased profits of machine productions. As
it was, the wealthy and enterprising and ruthless seized the new
opening, turned out a rapid flow of products, and of necessity
underbid the others in marketing their goods. The old customs and
regulations which had forbidden or limited free competition were
brushed away. New economic theories were developed which sanc-
tioned what was going on and secured the support of public opinion
and legislation for those who were driving the machine through the
framework of the social structure.

The distress of the displaced workers was terrible. In blind agony they mobbed the factories and destroyed the machines which were destroying them. But the men who owned the machines owned the law. In England the death penalty was put on the destruction of machinery. Sullenly the old masters had to bow their necks to the yoke. They had to leave their own shops and their old independence and come to the machine for work and bread. They had been masters; henceforth they had a master. The former companionship of master and workman, working together in the little shops, was gone. Two classes were created and a wide gulf separated them – on the one hand the employer, whose hands were white and whose power was great; on the other the wage-earner, who lived in a cottage and could only in rare and lessening instances hope to own a great shop with its costly machinery.

This disintegration of the old economic life has slowly spread, reaching one trade after the other, one nation after the other. To-day it is working its way in Russia and India. Longfellow, in his 'Village Blacksmith,' has described a master of the old kind. 'The smith, a mighty man was he, with strong and sinewy hands.' To-day one son of the smith is nailing machine-made shoes on with machine-made nails and repairing the iron-work of farmers which is wrought elsewhere. The other sons have gone into town and are factory hands. One worked in the fluff-filled air of a cotton-mill and slept in a dark bedroom. He died of consumption.

Thus went the old independence and the approximate equality of the old life. The old security disappeared too. A man could not even be sure of the bare wages which he received for his toil. The machine worked with such headlong speed that it glutted the market with its goods, and stopped its own wheels with the mass of its own output. Periodical prostrations of industry began with speculative production and a new kind of famine became familiar – the famine for work.

The machine required deftness rather than strength. The slender fingers of women and children sufficed for it and they were cheaper than men. So men were forced out of work by the competition of their own wives and children, and saw their loved ones wilt and die under the relentless drag of the machine. The saying that 'a man's foes shall be they of his own household' received a new application.

Under the old methods industry could be scattered over the

country. The machine now compelled population to settle about
it. It was the creator of the modern city. It piled the poor together
in crowded tenements at night and in unsanitary factories during the
day, and intensified all the diseases that come through crowding.
Poverty leaped forward simultaneously with wealth. From 1760 to
1818 the population of England increased seventy per cent.; the
poor relief increased five hundred per cent.

Here then we have the incredible paradox of modern life. The
instrument by which all humanity could rise from want and the fear
of want actually submerged a large part of the people in perpetual
want and fear. When wealth was multiplying beyond all human
precedent, an immense body of pauperism was growing up and
becoming chronic.

We live in this industrial age, an age of wonderful possibilities, yet
the incoming of which was fraught with such disastrous results.
Great social adjustments have taken place that have ameliorated distress and improved the condition of the working class, but there
remains a great gulf fixed between the capitalist-employer class and
the workers — a gulf that, despite efforts to bridge it, seems to be
ever widening.

As conservative an economist as Professor Cairns writes (*Leading
Principles*):

Unequal as is the distribution of wealth already in this country, the
tendency of industrial progress — on the supposition that the present
separation between industrial classes is maintained — is toward an
inequality greater still. The rich will be growing richer, and the poor
at least relatively poorer. It seems to me, apart altogether from the
question of the laborer's interest, that these are not conditions
which furnish a solid basis for a progressive social state; but, having
regard to that interest, I think the considerations adduced show that
the first and indispensable step toward any serious amendment of
the laborer's lot, is that he should be, in one way or another, lifted
out of the groove in which he at present works and placed in a position compatible with his becoming a sharer in equal proportion with
others in the general advantages arising from industrial progress.

In *The Social Unrest*, John Graham Brooks, although expressing
doubt as to the possibility of securing trustworthy statistics on

which to base such calculations, quotes Spahr's tables of the distribution of wealth in the United States:

Class	Families	Per cent	Average wealth	Aggregate wealth	Per cent
Rich	125,000	1.0	263,040	32,880,000,000	54.8
Middle	1,362,500	10.9	14,180	19,320,000,000	32.2
Poor	4,762,500	38.1	1,639	7,800,000,000	13.0
Very poor	6,250,000	50.0			

Whether or not these tables are anything like approximately
correct, it is very evident that there is something radically wrong
somewhere. Perhaps street corner agitators are not altogether wrong
when they denominate themselves 'wage slaves.' Benjamin Kidd
makes the following very significant statement: 'We are entering on a
new era. The political enfranchisement of the masses is well nigh
accomplished; the process which will occupy the next period will be
that of their social enfranchisement.'

We have been discussing some of the revolutionary effects of the
introduction of the power machine. One of these, the power of
organization, has in turn developed into the mightiest social force of
modern times. The capitalist-employer class has carried organization
far beyond the bounds of the individual factory, and now not only
industry but business of all kinds – commerce in general – is being
organized. On every hand we have great companies, extensive com-
bines, consolidated trusts, giant mergers and all-powerful
monopolies. An ever-lessening number of men control and reap the
profits of the leading industries, the great business houses, the railroad systems and the financial institutions. The rest of the population carry on the business and do the work, receiving larger or
smaller salaries and wages.

The business men have made and are still making a fight for
independence. The newer the country the more successfully this may
be carried on. But in face of such tremendous resources as are possessed
by the great organizations, capitulation is only a matter of time. The
most successful men become a part of the machine. The others go
under or maintain an existence in an essentially dependent relation.

In the workers' camp the forces have been slowly organizing;
a great mass can move but slowly. In the earlier factory days the

leaders recognized that individually they were helpless; that if they wished to sell their labor at a fair price they must resort to 'collective bargaining,' and so gradually arose the great trades and labor movement. A trade union, according to Mr. and Mrs. Sidney Webb (*History of Trade Unionism*), 'is a continuous association of wage-earners for the purpose of maintaining or improving the conditions of their employment.'

Unionism has already accomplished much. Factory acts, the reduction in the hours of labor and the establishment of a standard rate of wages have been brought about largely through pressure on the part of the Unions. In bringing about these reforms in England, Unionism has gradually become a political force and the Labor party has exerted an influence out of all proportion to the number of its representatives in Parliament.

But perhaps most important of all has been the training that the working class has received in self-government, together with a growing knowledge of the principles of economics, a sense of comradeship and a passionate idealism that one day will prove irresistible.

The Unions have made mistakes of course. Even leaders cannot see clearly and act dispassionately when they are hewing a way through an unknown jungle with the enemy harassing them at every forward movement. Then the leaders must carry the rank and file with them, and Unionism is the most democratic of all movements; this is its present weakness and its ultimate strength. In the final adjustment of the conflicting factors of the industrial situation and the social reconstruction that must inevitably take place, trades unionism will undoubtedly have a leading place.

Prof. Ely, recognized as an eminently sane and 'safe' authority, writes as follows:

The labor movement, then, in its broadest terms, is the effort of men to live the life of men. It is the systematic, organized struggle of the masses to attain primarily more leisure and larger economic resources; but that is not by any means all, because the end and purpose of it all is a richer existence for the toilers, and that with respect to mind, soul and body. Half conscious though it may be, the labor movement is a force pushing on towards the attainment of the purpose of humanity; in other words, the end of the true growth of mankind, namely, the full and harmonious development in each

'Homes' in our cities

1 The home of a new comer
2 Two families occupy each of these cottages
3 A family of eight and six roomers occupy half of this cottage
4 Broken windows, ill-fitted doors, cracks in the walls – 40 below zero

individual of all human faculties — the faculties of working, perceiving, knowing, loving — the development, in short, of whatever capabilities of good there may be in us. And this development of human powers in the individual is not to be entirely for self, but it is to be for the sake of their beneficent use in the service of one's fellows in a Christian civilization. It is for self and for others. It is the realization of the ethical aim expressed in that command which contains the secret of all true progress, 'Thou shalt love thy neighbor as thyself.' It is directed against oppression in every form because oppression carries with it the idea that persons or classes live, not to fulfil a destiny of their own, but primarily and chiefly for the sake of the welfare of other persons or classes. The true significance of the labor movement, on the contrary, lies in this. It is an attempt to bring to pass the idea of human development which has animated sages, prophets and poets of all ages; the idea that a time must come when warfare of all kinds shall cease, and when a peaceful organization of society shall find a place within its framework for the best growth of each personality and shall abolish all servitude in which one but subserves the other's gain.

The labor movement represents mankind as it is represented by no other manifestation of the life of the nations of the earth, because the vast majority of the race are laborers.

The following is the Platform of Principles laid down by the Trades and Labor Congress of Canada:

1 Free compulsory education.
2 Legal working day of eight hours, and six days to a week.
3 Government inspection of all industries.
4 The abolition of the contract system on all public works.
5 A minimum living wage, based on local conditions.
6 Public ownership of all franchises, such as railways, telegraphs, telephones, water-works, lighting, etc.
7 Tax reform by lessening taxation on industry and increasing it on land values.
8 Abolition of the Dominion Senate.
9 Exclusion of Chinese.
10 The Union Label to be placed on all manufactured goods, where practicable, and all government and municipal supplies.

11 Abolition of child labor by children under fourteen years of age, and of female labor in all branches of industrial life, such as mines, workshops, factories, etc.

12 Abolition of property qualification for all public offices.

13 Voluntary arbitration of labor disputes.

14 Proportional representation with grouped constituencies and abolition of municipal wards.

15 Direct legislation through the initiative and referendum.

16 Prohibition of prison labor in competition with free labor.

NB The Union Label. When firms carry on work under conditions satisfactory to labor they are permitted to use the Union Label on their products. All loyal unionists and their friends are urged to buy only those goods that carry the label.

The public is more or less familiar with the methods which are used in the warfare between the employer and the workers.

The employer takes the position: 'This is *my* business and I intend to run it. I will submit to no dictation as to wages, hours or conditions of work.' He stands for the open shop, where non-union men and union men have equal rights. He refuses to treat with or recognize the union. If hostilities commence he may 'lock out' union men or introduce non-union men to take the place of the striking workmen. He may black-list the strikers so that they will find it impossible to obtain work in any other factory. He may bring an injunction against the men's organization as being conspiracy in restraint of trade – an injunction disregard of which is contempt of court and punishable by imprisonment. His strike-breakers may goad the strikers or their sympathizers to violence and then he may urge that the militia be called out to quell the riot or protect his property. Industrial war passes into civil war.

The workers on their part claim – and the justice of their claim is being more clearly recognized – that they ought to have a voice in deciding the conditions under which they work. They insist on the recognition of the union. They may demand the closed shop, that is, that only union men be employed. As the only effective means of enforcing their demands they may resort to a strike. If non-union men – 'scabs,' as they are called – are brought in, they establish a system of espionage, seeking to win over or to intimidate the strike-breakers. They may induce allied trades to call a sympathetic strike.

In excitement or desperation they may resort to violence that often ends in bloodshed and always in bitterness.

Finally one side may yield, or there may be an arbitration followed by some sort of compromise. Surely a stupidly wasteful method entailing great inconvenience to the public, disorganization to the industry and hardship to the men — loss all around!

And all this might often be saved by a joint agreement by which the interests alike of the employer, the worker and the public would be conserved.

John Graham Brooks writes: 'For that trouble-breeding portion of industry here discussed the joint agreement is all that any "solution" can be, namely, the next best practical step toward a rational industrial method. These agreements are not of universal application. They apply at points where unionism is inevitable, where the wage system is under such a strain as to require modification in the direction of a more democratized management. Every scheme that is not inherently educational is worthless, because the clash of the trust and the trade union is raising new issues for which an enlarged social morality is necessary.'

Advanced social legislation in Germany, constructive movements in England, radical experiments in Australia and New Zealand should be carefully studied. Of special interest to us is the working out of our own Industrial Disputes Act. But into these fields we cannot enter. At every turn we meet with innumerable problems whose solution will require the best thought of our strongest men.

What the final solution will be and how it is to be attained none but a prophet can tell. There are those who advocate voluntary co-operative effort by which the profits of middlemen and the gains of speculators will be eliminated, that is, will be retained by the workers as producers or saved by them as consumers. Many most interesting and successful experiments along these lines have been carried on in England, though probably any great extension of this movement is impracticable.

Next comes the plan of public ownership. In England great municipal enterprises have been remarkably successful and on the Continent government-owned railroads have for years been considered as legitimate an institution as is our postal system. In America, municipal ownership of a certain class of public enterprises is growing in favor; but determined opposition develops when it is proposed to extend, to any marked degree, the sphere of public activity to those industries that are now carried on by private enterprises.

Public control by means of taxation has many advocates. The disciples of Henry George believe that if the Single Tax were adopted special privileges would be abolished and all would have a fair chance. The right of the public to what has been termed 'the unearned increment' must be conceded in theory though difficult to secure in practice. The most notable advance along this line was that made by Lloyd-George in his now famous Budget.

Other reformers, especially on this continent, advocate Government control by means of detailed legislation and careful supervision. Roosevelt would control the trusts. Here in Canada our Railway Commission, with its large powers, is a distinct advance in subordinating the selfish interests of a corporation to the welfare of the public generally.

Then there are those who utterly despair of any real reformation of the present system. There must come a complete revolution in our economic and social system. Individualistic competition must be replaced by Socialistic co-operation.

Many of our profound thinkers believe that the real difficulty is a moral one, that so long as men are essentially selfish no scheme, however attractive, can accomplish much. Men must be educated to altruism, or their hearts changed, before our social evils will disappear.

As Shailer Mathews has pointed out, 'the age does not see its way clearly.' But we may see in which quarter the light is breaking and push forward in that direction even though we have many a stumble and fall. We ourselves confess to a certain eclecticism. Each of these proposed solutions contains a measure of truth. Perhaps the final result will show that none of them is adequate and that the line of development will be the resultant of many social forces, some of which are still largely latent.

We hold firmly that personal morality is the basis of public morality and yet admit that the morality of the community, as expressed in its customs and institutions, is the most potent factor in determining the morality of the individual. We dream of a socialistic state and yet sympathize with Mr. Brooks when he says that 'the Mecca of the Co-operative Commonwealth is not to be reached by setting class against class, but by bearing common burdens through toilsome stages along which all who wish well to their fellows can journey together.' If there *must* be a fight then it is a fight for the rights of the many weak against the privileges of the strong few and we stand with the many weak. We believe in opportunism and compromise in securing practical reforms, but never when they involve the abandonment of the hope of attaining the ultimate goal, or the sacrifice of vital principles.

Let me again give a lengthy quotation from Hunter, who summarizes his conclusions as to conditions in the United States and suggests lines of remedial action. These paragraphs open up the whole field of social reform.

How far are these conditions yet true of Canada and how many of the suggestions are immediately practicable in our own city?

There are probably in fairly prosperous years no less than 10,000,000 persons in poverty; that is to say, underfed, underclothed and poorly housed. Of these, 4,000,000 persons are public paupers. Over 2,000,000 working-men are unemployed from four to six months in the year. About 500,000 male immigrants arrive yearly and seek work in the very districts where unemployment is greatest. Nearly half of the families in the country are propertyless. Over 1,700,000 little children are forced to become wage-earners when they should be in school. About 5,000,000 women find it necessary to work and about 2,000,000 are employed in factories, mills, etc. Probably no less than 1,000,000 workers are injured or killed each year while doing their work and about 10,000,000 of the persons now living will, if the present ratio is kept up, die of the preventable disease tuberculosis. We know that many workmen are overworked and underpaid. We know in a general way that unnecessary disease is far too prevalent. We know some of the insanitary evils of tenements and factories; we know of the neglect of the street child, the aged, the infirm, the crippled. Furthermore, we are beginning to realize the monstrous injustice of compelling those who are unemployed, who are injured in industry, who have acquired diseases due to their occupation, or who have been made widows or orphans by industrial accidents, to become paupers in order that they may be housed, fed and clothed. Something is known concerning these problems of poverty, and some of them at least are possible of remedy.

To deal with these specific problems, I have elsewhere mentioned some reforms which seem to me preventive in their nature. They contemplate mainly such legislative action as may enforce upon the entire country certain minimum standards of working and of living conditions. They would make all tenements and factories sanitary; they would regulate the hours of work, especially for women and children; they would regulate and supervise dangerous trades; they would institute all necessary measures to stamp out unnecessary disease and to prevent unnecessary death; they would prohibit entirely child labor; they would institute all necessary educational and recreational institutions to replace the social and educational losses of the home and the domestic workshop; they would perfect, as far as possible, legislation and institutions to make industry pay the necessary and legitimate cost of producing and maintaining efficient laborers; they would institute on the lines of foreign experience, measures to compensate labor for enforced seasons of idleness due to sickness, old age, lack of work, or other causes beyond the control of the workman; they would prevent parasitism on the part of either the consumer or the producer, and charge up the full costs of labor in production to the beneficiary, instead of compelling the worker at certain times to enforce his demand for maintenance through the tax rate and by becoming a pauper; they would restrict the power of employer and of shipowner to stimulate for purely selfish ends an excessive immigration and in this way to beat down wages and to increase unemployment.

REFERENCES

'The Social Unrest'
John Graham Brooks. New York: Grosset & Dunlap
'Social Solutions'
Thomas C. Hall. New York: Eaton & Mains
'Poverty'
Robert Hunter. New York: The Macmillan Co.
'Life and Labor of the People in London'
Charles Booth. New York: The Macmillan Co.
'Problems of Poverty'
John A. Hobson. London: Methuen & Co.

'The Labor Movement in America'
Richard T Ely. New York: The Macmillan Co.
'History of Trades Unionism'
Sidney and Beatrice Webb. New York: Longmans, Green & Co.
'The Canadian Industrial Disputes Act'
Adam Shortt. Pub. American Economic Association
'The Labor Movement in Australasia'
Victor S. Clark. Westminster: Archibald, Constable & Co.
'Socialism'
John Spargo. New York: The Macmillan Co.
'Socialism and Government'
J. Ramsay MacDonald. London: T. C. and E. C. Jack
'Organized Labor'
John Mitchell. Philadelphia: American Book and Bible House

Chapter 4

The undermining of the home

Where there are no homes there will be no nation.

Veiller

Oh, room for the lamb in the meadow,
   And room for the bird on the tree!
But here, in stern poverty's shadow,
   No room, hapless baby! for thee.

E. M. Milne

REPLACING HOME AND NATURE
We forget that the home is, for the working people, a few rooms in a crowded, yardless tenement, and that the individual parent cannot save the child from the deadening and aimless play of the city's streets. He may not give him work with tools, for there is no room in the tenement where the child can work; the parent may not watch him at his play, for he is in a factory, and not in a home workshop or in the neighboring fields. In a word, the working-man cannot, as things now are, supervise the play of his child. We must, therefore, go farther than to liberate the child from slavery; we must see that his hours of freedom are utilized in those kinds of recreation and occupation which shall most develop him.

Hunter

IN OUR city life many forces are at work tending to change materially the character of the home.

All must recognize the growing numbers of homeless people. Think of our boarding-house population of young business men and women. Whole sections of the central residential districts of our cities are occupied by this class. The majority, at least, of the younger people come from the country or from towns and villages attracted by the greater possibilities of the city. Their 'home' consists of a bed-room, probably shared with a friend, and perhaps the use of a common parlor, though the latter is becoming the exception. Meals – at least the noon meals – are taken at a restaurant. The evenings must be spent somewhere, probably as many as possible at the cheap theatre. There you have it – sleep, eat, work, put in the time. They are largely free from responsibilities of home or business, for no one much cares how they come or go and much of their work is mere routine in a business in which they have little interest or prospects. What an existence! And yet this is more or less the life of thousands of our young people.

Freed from old restraints and without any great ambition, is it any wonder that many young men make shipwreck of their lives? Why not set up homes of their own? There are many reasons. The care-free life has its attractions and marriage is, in thought, continually postponed. The financial question is probably the most serious. Standards of living, as well as cost of living, are high. It is no light undertaking to establish and maintain a home on the salary received by the ordinary clerk. The effect of business life upon our girls is decidedly marked.

A business-girl friend has given me the profit and loss account. 'On the one side business life may broaden a girl's outlook on life, create a spirit of worthy independence, give her a chance to develop, make her self-reliant, teach her economy, system and thrift, bring her into touch with all kinds of people and give her a splendid knowledge of human nature. On the other side, it tends to destroy her womanliness, to lower her ideals, to destroy her individuality and break down her health. It exposes her to severe temptations and makes her less anxious to assume the duties of wife and mother.'

Housing a lower grade of workers we have the lodging-house of all degrees of cheapness. Our industries and our constructive works call for large armies of unskilled workers. The very nature of their work,

A plea for playgrounds
Front and back views of some Toronto homes

seasonal, shifting and intermittent, demands that they be more or less a mobile force without the incumbrances of a fixed home and a family. Then, the wages paid, making allowance for loss of time, are such that, without being supplemented by earnings of wife or children, it is impossible to make and keep a home. This ill-paid, aimless, roving life reacts upon the men and is creating a large and well-recognized class – 'the homeless man.' The homeless man lives with a crowd, similarly situated, in a large, rough boarding-house. His bed and meals, with a little for clothes, form his expense budget. He could save something, of course – many do. But with a large number there is little to encourage them. The hope of independence is remote and problematical. Coarse pleasures abound on every hand. What would you do if you had to live like this? (See illustration, p. 141.)

The following extracts from the first annual report of The Associated Charities of the City of Winnipeg, while they deal with merely the homeless men who have been in need of charitable help, throw a valuable side-light on the whole class:

Careful records were taken of the cases dealt with and interesting statistics have been drawn from 660 cases, the most important features of which are here set forth.

Nationality by birth

	Per cent		Per cent
English	57.61	Canadian	9.09
Scotch	16.96	U.S.A.	1.81
Irish	8.93	German	1.36
Welsh	1.06	Other foreign	3.18
	———		———
British Isles	84.56		15.44

The birth statistics endorse at first sight the views so often expressed in Canada that the immigrant from Great Britain, and from England in particular, is slow to adapt himself to Canadian life. The higher percentage of Anglo-Saxons leads one to enquire why the foreigners do not become dependent. The answer is easy: The normal standard of living of the Anglo-Saxon is far more costly than that of the foreigner.

On the one hand we find the Anglo-Saxon lodging, so long as funds hold out, at the dollar-a-day hotel; on the other hand we find the foreigners swarming, during winter months, as cheap boarders into already overcrowded family homes. Even in their vices they are respectively extravagant and economical. The Anglo-Saxon patronizes the bar-room and the house of ill-fame, whilst the foreigners club together to purchase drink, barrels at a time, and satisfy their passions indiscriminately amongst their women-folk ...

Though no exact record of the direct or indirect cause of destitution was made, we feel satisfied that in not less than 80 per cent. of the cases intemperance was an important factor; certainly the cases of habitual intemperance were in the minority; seasonal labor produces seasonal intemperance, and time and time again hard-earned summer's wages disappeared in a few days in, or through, excessive drinking ...

Some factors seem so clearly responsible for this condition of affairs that we venture to record them:

The lack of good, attractive accommodation for casual and seasonal laborers visiting Winnipeg 'between jobs,' such as would compete with the 'dollar-a-day' licensed houses, which however well conducted prove a veritable death-trap to the seasonal laborer who visits the city with an accumulation of wages. For this evil we see a remedy in the establishment of 'Temperance Hotels' and the stricter enforcement of the Liquor License Law, which forbids the serving of intoxicating liquor to a man already under its influence.

The absence of healthy amusement, attractions, and places for social intercourse to compete with *camaraderie* of the 'bar-room' and the allurement of the house of ill-fame. Men of the class we speak of do not use the Carnegie Free Library — they require a place to sit and chat and smoke, with rooms set aside for board-games and reading; nor must the light refreshment bar be omitted or the desire for 'treating' will lead the men to the saloon. In other words, the city wants a Y.M.C.A. for working laborers.

We come nearer to the home in the case of working girls, many of whom actually live in their own homes or with friends. Girls employed in domestic service form a class by themselves; it is to be greatly regretted that these girls, whose work brings them into such close association with homes, should be homeless, often having to resort to the street as the only possible place in which to meet a friend. With long hours and inferior social status it is little wonder that girls are glad to escape from housework to the more independent if worse-paid work in shops and factories. Here we find a life that is full of temptations, and only girls of fine instincts, high character and good training will escape a sad coarsening as the months go on. The place which the majority of these factory girls call home, even though it is where their parents live, has little to attract. There is little accommodation, no comforts, no privacy. The girls must go out for their pleasures. Home is, for all practical purposes, but the cheapest of boarding-houses.

Of those who may lay claim to homes in the city, comparatively few own them. Land is so high that only the well-to-do can hope to secure property of their own. In Canada we are just passing out of the village stage, but already we have in the rapid rise of values and rents an indication of what is coming. Of the United States Dr. Strong, says: 'In the six cities of 500,000 inhabitants or more, the average percentage who owned their homes was 21.4, while in Manhattan and Bronx, where population is densest, the proportion drops to 5.9. In our Assembly district, out of 14,000 homes, only 56 were owned by those who occupied them, and of these only 14 were unencumbered – one in a thousand.'

The detached house in the middle of the lot with its front and back gardens and lawns is becoming for the majority in our own cities a dream of the past. Apartment houses, tenements, rooming houses, are going up in every direction. Among the poorer classes, the tenements are more simply constructed. An old residence is divided into suites, or more simply still, each room becomes a residence. According to Mr. Charles Booth, in London there are 2,257,000 people who singly or in companies live in one room – sleeping, cooking, eating, bathing, if at all, within the same four walls.

To come nearer home. At the tenth Canadian Conference of Charities and Correction, Mr. J. J. Kelso, speaking of conditions in Toronto, said:

I pass up and down through the central district a great deal and have often been struck with the haphazard way in which people are allowed to live. Not long ago, I was going down one of these streets

and I saw a crowd of Italians hurrying into a small building. It
seemed as if the whole street was going in. I enquired of a little girl
standing by, what was the matter, and she said: 'Those are only the
men going to dinner!' The house would probably not have more
than five rooms and there were at least 25 to 30 of these men living
there. On another occasion I went through the foreign district after
11 o'clock at night with one of the City Officers, and in every room
we went to there were at least four to six persons sleeping, and there
were no less than three cottages or houses, one behind the other, in
this same overcrowded condition. Often the better class of citizens
do not know what is going on, so these wretched social conditions
are allowed to grow until they become well-nigh intolerable. Many
will tell you that we in Toronto are free from slums, but they are
only shutting their eyes to evils that exist. Some of these vile hovels
are old cottages built 60 years ago and not improved in any way
since – floors sunk, walls out of shape, plaster off, windows broken,
and yet these houses are bringing to their owners about four to six
times the rent that was paid many years ago when they were in good
order. Poor unfortunate people pay $8 and $10 a month for one or
two rooms, with no closet, but only vile cesspools used by all alike.
They are enough to infect the city, and our Health Department
ought to order the pulling down of such places.

Altogether aside from the ownership of the building it is no light
struggle for the majority of city-dwellers to furnish and maintain the
home. R. C. Chapin states after a careful study of the standard of
living among working-men's families in New York City: 'It seems
safe to conclude that an income under $800 is not enough to permit
the maintenance of a normal standard. On the other hand an income
of $900 or over probably permits the maintenance of a normal
standard at least so far as the physical man is concerned.'
But man does not live by bread alone. The so-called 'culture
wants' are as imperative as the physical. A home is more than an
eating and sleeping house. How then keep up a home, as many are
forced to do, on much less than the minimum $900?
Often this can be done by the ordinary family income being
supplemented by the earnings of the wife and children, and this,
alas, too often means the sacrifice of the best things that home life
should yield.

When the mother is absent from the home the children are sadly neglected. The younger children suffer physically; the elder ones through lack of discipline often become utterly unmanageable and thus qualify for a life of crime. It ought to be a fixed rule with social workers that such arrangements should be made as would leave the mother free to care for her home and children.

Another fixed rule ought to be the prohibition of any work by a

OUR SCHOOLS SHOW MANY NATIONALITIES

Nationalities	Totals	Grades						
		i	ii	iii	iv	v	vi	vii
Canadian	45	12	4	3	6	3	12	5
English	61	12	12	6	19	4	5	3
Irish	9	1	–	2	2	2	2	–
Scotch	14	3	2	1	3	3	2	–
American	10	1	–	1	2	2	2	2
Swedish	16	4	4	3	5	–	–	–
Norwegian	13	6	2	1	4	–	–	–
Icelandic	1	1	–	–	–	–	–	–
German	135	85	14	13	18	2	3	–
Austrian	7	1	–	2	4	–	–	–
Russian	23	21	–	2	–	–	–	–
Polish	43	22	5	2	7	4	2	1
Galician	9	4	1	4	–	–	–	–
Bohemian	7	4	2	1	–	–	–	–
Jewish (Russian)	95	45	22	13	7	2	5	1
Jewish (all others)	102	52	20	5	19	3	2	1
	590	274	88	59	96	25	35	13

The above table shows the nationalities represented in one of the public schools of Winnipeg. Note the attendance in the several grades, there being only 13 pupils in grade vii.

IN MANITOBA
From 26,705 to 40,707 Children of School Age are not attending any school.
Over ¼ of the Rural Schools are Bi-Lingual.

child that would in any way mortgage his future. Often children are kept from school and set to work at a very young age. Frequently health is impaired, morals corrupted and educational opportunities forever lost. Even sickness in the family cannot justify such a sacrifice. The community cannot afford to allow its future citizens to be weaklings or illiterates or criminals.

An investigation recently made among factory girls in Winnipeg in connection with the work of the Manitoba Government Commission on Technical Education yielded some interesting information:

Of the group of 165 girls interviewed:
 2 left school at the age of 16
15 left school at the age of 15
45 left school at the age of 14
34 left school at the age of 13
 8 left school at the age of 12
 3 left school at the age of 11
 1 left school at the age of 8
 9 never attended school
48 did not give information

Grade reached in Winnipeg Public Schools:
 4 reached Grade 8
10 reached Grade 7
 9 reached Grade 6
17 reached Grade 5
11 reached Grade 4
10 reached Grade 3
 5 reached Grade 2
 2 reached Grade 1

43 did not attend school since coming to this country
29 attended Parish Schools
 5 attended school in another town
 2 attended night school only

Why they left school:
58 because of hard circumstances at home
19 lacked ambition and were tired of work

10 owing to sickness at home
 9 discouragement — not allowed to attend regularly
 9 did not desire to start again in this country
 7 reached highest grade in public school
 2 no higher grade in country school
 1 on account of defective eyesight

One of the principals of the public schools states: 'I have noted during the past five years that many children leave school to go to work long before they are physically fit or have any adequate preparation for their life work. Very few children in our district complete the eighth grade in school (i.e., the public school course). They go to work in stores, box factories, breweries and as messenger and office boys. Many girls and boys are kept at home to mind younger children while the parents are out working. It is a sad fact, but it seems necessary that in order to maintain the existence of a family the mother must go out to work rather than care for her children. This is the source of much truancy and juvenile crime.'

Laws providing for compulsory education and forbidding child labor ought to be enacted in every Province in Canada. Every boy and girl should have a chance in life.

From a sheaf of reports from Mission visitors, I have selected the following as typical descriptions of many of the poorer 'homes' of our cities. What good thing can be expected to come from such conditions?

A small room at the back, very crowded, with double bed, small stove and table. The air was very, very bad and both door and window were kept tightly closed. Father was out looking for work. The mother was out washing. The stove was dirty and piled up with dirty pots and kettles. The table showed signs of breakfast — dirty granite dishes and spoons, two whisky bottles and part of a loaf of bread from which the cat was now having its breakfast.

The bed was like all the beds in this class of home — mattress covered by an old gray blanket, two big, dirty-looking pillows and some old clothes. This was the children's playground, for there was no floor space uncovered. Under the bed we noticed some cooking utensils, white-wash brush, an axe, spade, a dozen or more empty bottles, some clothing and a sack of bread.

If ignorance breeds vice, what of these children?

Boys of school age on the street
Girls and boys of school age in a factory

Shack — one room and a lean-to. Furniture — two beds, a bunk, stove, bench, two chairs, table, barrel of sauerkraut. Everything very dirty. Two families lived here. Women were dirty, unkempt, bare-footed, half-clothed. Children wore only print slips. The baby was in swaddling clothes and was lying in a cradle made of sacking suspended from the ceiling by ropes at the corners. The mother could lie in bed and rock the cradle above her. The supper was on the table — a bowl of warmed-over potatoes for each person, part of a loaf of brown bread, a bottle of beer.

Shack. Family consisted of father, mother, eight children. Deaconess was in a car one day in December when two half-clad, dirty children got in. They had no tickets and when the conductor proceeded to put them off, she paid the fares and took the children to the Mission supply room and sent them home clean and warmly clad. Two days later she went to the address given by the children and found the children dressed as before, just starting for town. The parents had a strong disinclination to work and sent the children out with a well-worded story to appeal to the tender-hearted of Winnipeg. The home was very dirty, the children badly-trained and not sufficiently nourished. Work was procured for both father and mother and when pressure was brought to bear upon them to make them provide for the needs of their family and educate their children, they hurriedly left town.

When we come to the life in the home many questions crowd themselves upon our attention. Of primary importance is the capability of the home-maker — the wife and mother. Many girls when they enter upon married life have absolutely no knowledge or experience or ideals with regard to home-making. They have not been trained in cooking or housekeeping. They have little idea of how to 'manage' — and in many working-men's homes the financial arrangements are left entirely to the wife. They have not been instructed in the simplest laws of hygiene or procreation. They are quite ignorant as to the approved methods of child-feeding or child-training. The wonder is that so many in spite of their serious handicaps 'make good' and succeed in establishing good homes. The pity of it is that so many fail. Unhappy home life, infant mortality, disease, shiftlessness, poverty, the unmanageableness of children and

their consequent evil careers, much of all this could be prevented if
girls – yes, and boys – could be given a good, common-sense training in the duties of home-making.

In a chapter on the 'Blighting of the Babies,' Spargo in *The Bitter
Cry of the Children* deals with the effects upon the children of the
ignorance of the mothers and some of the causes of this ignorance:

One poor woman whose little child was ailing became very irate
when a lady visitor ventured to offer her some advice concerning the
child's clothing and food, and soundly berated her would-be adviser.
'You talk to me about how to look after my baby,' she cried. 'Why,
I guess I know more about it than you do. I've buried nine already.'
It is not the naive humor of the poor woman's wrath that is most
significant, but the grim tragic pathos back of it. These four words,
'I've buried nine already,' tell more eloquently than could a hundred
learned essays or polished orations the vastness of civilization's
failure. For surely we may not regard it as anything but failure so
long as women who have borne eleven children into the world, as
had this one, can say 'I've buried nine already!'

But circular letters and lady visitors will not solve the problem of
maternal ignorance; such methods can only skim the surface of the
evil. This ignorance on the part of mothers, of which the babies are
victims, is deeply rooted in the soil of those economic conditions
which constitute poverty in the broadest sense of the term, though
there may be no destitution or absolute want. It is not poverty in
the narrow sense of the lack of the material necessities of life, but
rather a condition in which these are obtainable only by the concentrated efforts of all members of the family able to contribute
anything and to the exclusion of all else in life. Young girls who go
to work in shops and factories as soon as they are old enough to
obtain employment continue working up to within a few days of
marriage, and not infrequently return to work for some time after
marriage. Especially is this true of girls employed in mills and
factories; their male acquaintances are for the most part fellow
workers and marriages between them are numerous. Where many
women are employed, men's wages are, as a consequence, almost
invariably low, with the result that after marriage it is as necessary
that the woman should work as it was before.

When the years which under more favored conditions would have been spent at home in preparation for the duties of wifehood and motherhood are spent behind the counter, at the bench, or amid the whirl of machinery in the factory, it is scarcely to be wondered at that the knowledge of domestic economy is scant among them and that so many utterly fail as wives and mothers. Deprived of the opportunities of helping their mothers with the housework and cooking and the care of the younger children, marriage finds them ill-equipped; too often they are slaves to the frying-pan, or to the stores where cooked food may be bought in small quantities. Bad cooking, extravagance and mismanagement are incidental to our modern industrial conditions.

In the matter of home training, especially that of girls, I have the following statement from one of our deaconesses who has had wide experience:

I have found case after case where parents have lost entire control of their children and unless some extreme measures are taken one can see nothing ahead of these children but ruin. We believe the fault is more often with the parents than with the children themselves. In a great many homes the father and mother disagree as to how a child shall be guided and controlled and the child generally maps out a course for itself. At five, six and seven years of age we have known children openly refuse to obey their parents, lie to them, steal from them, stay away for hours without the parents' knowledge or permission. From the age of 12 upward we have known of both boys and girls staying away all night and sometimes longer without the permission of parents. When you talk to the parents and advise them to take the matter up with the officers of the Juvenile Court they become indignant and tell you their children are not bad. Many mothers will screen the children's guilt from the father to avoid unpleasantness or a whipping for the child.

The care and home training of girls is not sufficiently attended to by mothers. In many homes the mothers are so busy attending to the care of the babies and the household that the older girls are left free at the very period of their lives when they need the companionship and care of a mother. In many cases the girls have both boy and girl friends quite unknown to the parents. They go to parks, rinks, dance halls, etc., and come home at 11, 12, and often much later with men they have met at these places. The parents often do not even inquire with whom or where they have been. In other cases the parents become angry and scold the girl until the home is unbearable and when she escapes the door is locked and she may climb through a window, stay with friends, or spend the night as she pleases.

Another cause of the downfall of so many girls is dress. Many mothers will work far into the night sewing for their girls in order that they may be dressed 'as good as other girls.' It is made the subject of constant conversation, the cast-off finery of the south-end ladies is procured from some second-hand store, colored or cleaned, in order that 'my girl will have everything she needs.' Then since there are not admiring friends enough at home she is sent or allowed to walk the street in the evening to 'show off,' and the end is what might be expected.

Bessie is a girl of this class. Her mother kept her at school until she was thirteen, and then sent her to a factory to work. All went well for a time. Everybody told her how pretty she was and how becomingly she was dressed. Her earnings went to clothe her, and when they failed her devoted mother and sisters gave her extras. Every night she arrayed herself in her dainty dresses the mother had spent so many hours over, and went to visit her friends, or to the theatre. Few questions were asked and they were easily answered. At fifteen she decided she would stay home with her mother and help only in the home. The sisters still supported her and she got up later each morning.

One night the girl remained away all night, but the mother was not alarmed and said she must be with friends. Later an officer called to tell her the girl was in the police station for being on the street at 3 a.m., in questionable company.

A few months later the girl asked permission to visit a friend in the country. She was seen no more — her downfall was complete!

The fact is that in our city life we are facing conditions that are undermining the home. So little is this understood and yet so important are the consequences that I venture to give at length a most admirable treatment of the whole subject. This is taken from Hunter's work on *Poverty* previously quoted, which we should like to induce everyone to read.

A few decades ago in England and America, practically the entire life of parents and children — whether working, playing, or learning —

was in and about the home, and even now in certain backward
industrial countries this is likewise true. The mass of people lived in
small towns, or hamlets, as they might better be called, since that
word in itself conveys the idea of home. There were a few large
towns, but most of the population was grouped in these small rural
communities. Nearly all work was done by hand-manufacture.
Horse-power, water-power, and hand-power were the bases of the
industry. The home fields raised the foodstuffs; killing, cooking,
baking, brewing, smithing, forging, spinning, and weaving were home
occupations. The home had its own water supply; the home supplied
its own defence; the home took precautions against disease and
cared for the sick and even the insane. Social gatherings took place
in the fields near the home or in the house itself. The children
received practically their entire education either in the home or in
the adjoining fields. Certainly in those days the child received his
best education under the supervision of his own parents. The entire
schooling, which was necessarily restricted to the teaching of the
three R's, did not average in 1800 more than eighty-two days for
each person. The children were nearly always in the sight of their
parents. Both parents worked, and the children worked also; but the
parents could stop in their work at any time for the purpose of
instructing the children. In a word, the home was the centre of the
moral, educational, industrial and social life.

In most of the countries of Western Europe and America, this is
now all changed. Except in a few belated industries, the domestic
workshop no longer exists, even in the country; industrial processes,
except of course, agriculture, are now carried on by large, well-
organized groups of employees, in offices, factories, mills, and
mines, sometimes of enormous size. Steam and electricity have
displaced hand, water and horse power, as the motive forces of
industry. The individual workshop has given way to large co-
operative methods of work. Hamlets have grown into factory towns,
and the towns into cities. Millions of people in all parts of Western
Europe have emigrated from their homes and fields in the rural
districts to the crowded centres of industry. We have now, on an
enormous scale, co-operative production, a minutely organized
division of labor and great aggregations of working people laboring
together in the houses of industry and dwelling together in the huge
tenements of our cities. No revolution was ever before known that

so completely and rapidly revolutionized the life and work of the people as this one of the last century.

When this revolution brought into the world large cities and a new industrial life, it at the same time destroyed what has been described as the Home. In our largest cities *this* home no longer exists. The economic development of the last hundred years has destroyed it and left in its stead a mere shadow of what once was the source of all things essential to the world. The mills, factories, abattoirs, breweries and bakeries took from the home the various trades, the state supplied the defence, and the city the water supply; the sanitarium, the surgeon, and the alienist took precaution against disease and replaced home remedies by skilled practice and medical science; the sick have hospital care, the schools undertake the instruction of the child, and the factory, etc., the technical training. The home is now a few rooms in a crowded tenement or apartment house. The fields have diminished to the commons, the commons to yards, and the yards to courts and light shafts; the tenement has become yardless. Little or nothing has replaced the social losses of the home, and the same may be said of the possibilities for recreation, which were lost with the fields and commons. A few settlements have endeavored to supply opportunities for keeping alive the neighborhood feeling; a few playgrounds have come to supply the recreative needs; but the losses have been serious and as yet there are no sufficient substitutes. The rapidity with which this revolution has occurred is almost unbelievable. There are men now living who have seen the working out of the whole industrial process.

Every one of these changes has had its effect upon the child. Although, in the working out of this process, the child was never thought of, the revolution has vitally changed the environment and conditions of child life. We are in an era of great cities, and in a few years the mass of our population will live in cities. In these changes from the home to the factory, from the cottage to the tenement, and from the country to the city, the needs of childhood have been forgotten. Imagine a child in a great city, cities that are, as Ruskin has said, 'mere crowded masses of store and warehouse and counter, and therefore to the rest of the world what the larder and cellar are to the private house; cities in which the object of men is not life, but labor; and in which all chief magnitude of edifice is to enclose machinery; cities in which the streets are not the avenues for the

passing and procession of a happy people, but the drains for the
discharge of a tormented mob, in which the only object in reaching
any spot is to be transferred to another; in which existence becomes
mere transition, and every creature is only one atom in a drift of
human dust and current of interchanging particles, circulating here
by tunnels underground, and there by tubes in the air.'

In the scramble to re-adjust ourselves to the cities and to this new
industrial life, built up as a result of steam and electricity, the child
has been forgotten. To a very large extent he has been left to re-
adjust himself, and the result is a series of really appalling problems.
His father now leaves the home and goes to the factory; he may not
watch his father at work or work with him – and it would not be
good for him if he could – until he himself is old enough to become
a laborer. He is in the city instead of in the country. He has lost the
playgrounds which nature lavishly furnished – the hills, valleys,
woodland, the thousand varieties of plants and animals, the streams,
the blue sky over all, even the starry night. Bored by the homeless
tenement, he finds himself on an asphalt pavement, in a crowded
street, amid roars of excitement – in a playground alive with
business with which he must not interfere. But he plays; the street is
interesting, garbage boxes and lamp-posts have a place in his games,
and the child is happy, God bless him.

These changes in the living and working conditions of the people
and these changes in the environment of the child demand new
agencies for the care of the child, and a series of important readjust-
ments of the social and educational institutions to the altered
economic conditions. Certain social institutions have already re-
adjusted themselves, but the distinctly educational institutions have
been slow to change. All institutions for the common good undertaken by the community have developed more slowly than those
institutions which have been initiated by individuals for the purpose
of gaining profits. Parks, playgrounds, baths, recreation centres,
athletic fields, gymnasia, social halls, play centres, creches, the social
use of schools and school excursions to the country, have developed
more slowly than saloons, theatres, public dance halls, rapid transit,
etc., because there is no possibility of large profits in developing the
former institutions, so necessary especially to the children. The great
cities need social statesmen who, seeing the evils of child life, will
bring about, through public agencies, the new institutions required

to save the rising generations from crime, street life, physical degeneration, and all the other evil results of the worst phases of city life.

A CHRISTMAS PRAYER FOR CHILDREN WHO WORK
'O Thou, Great Father of the weak, lay Thy hand tenderly on all the little children on earth and bless them. Bless our own children who are the life of our life and who have become the heart of our heart. Bless every little child friend who has leaned against our knee and refreshed our soul by its smiling trustfulness. Be good to all children who crave in vain for human love, or for flowers and water, and the sweet breast of nature. But bless with a three-fold blessing the young lives whose slender shoulders are already bowed beneath the yoke of toil and whose glad growth is being stunted forever. Let not their little bodies be utterly sapped, and their minds given over to stupidity and the vices of an empty soul. We have all jointly deserved the mill-stone of Thy wrath for making these little ones to stumble and fall. Grant all employers of labor stout hearts to refuse enrichment at such a price. Grant to all the citizens and officers of states which now permit this wrong the grace of holy anger. Help us to realize that every child in our nation is in very truth our child, a member of our great family. By the Holy Child that nestled in Mary's bosom, by the memories of our own childhood's joys and sorrows, by the sacred possibilities that slumber in every child, we beseech Thee to save us from killing the sweetness of young life by the greed of gain.'
                          Walter Rauschenbusch, in the *American Magazine*

REFERENCES

'The Bitter Cry of the Children'
John Spargo. New York: Young People's Missionary Movement
'The Peril of the Home'
Jacob Riis. New York: Young People's Missionary Movement
'The Leaven in a Great City'
Lillian W. Betts. New York: Young People's Missionary Movement
'Americans in Process'
Robert A. Woods. Boston: Houghton, Mifflin Co.
'The Spirit of Youth and the City Streets'
Jane Addams. New York: The Macmillan Co.

'The Standard of Living Among Workingmen's Families in New
York City'
R. C. Chapin. New York: Charities Publication Committee
'Women and the Trades'
Elizabeth B. Butler. New York: Charities Publication Committee
Reports of Social Workers offer abundant material

Chapter 5

Social life

And the streets of the city shall be full of boys and girls playing in the streets thereof.

Zech

America is God's Crucible, the great Melting Pot where all the races of Europe are melting and reforming! Here you stand, good folk, think I, when I see them at Ellis Island, here you stand in your fifty groups, with your fifty languages and histories, and your fifty blood hatreds and rivalries. But you won't be long like that, brothers, for these are the fires of God you've come to — these are the fires of God. A fig for your feuds and vendettas! Germans and Frenchmen, Irishmen and Englishmen, Jews and Russians — into the Crucible with you all! God is making the American.

Israel Zangwill

CONFESSEDLY one is at a loss to know where to begin in entering upon a field so large and varied and with limits so vaguely defined. There are so many kinds of social life – the life in the home, in the workshop, on the street, at the church, in the social club, at the places of public amusement – wherever men and women congregate. Each of these again is different in each social class. Contrast the social life in the home of the mechanic with that in the residence of the prosperous business man; the greetings in the synagogue with the fellowship of the class meeting; the 'society' club with the fraternal organization or the saloon circle. Then above all with our immigrant population we have imported the varying social life of half the countries of Europe and Asia; Briton and Slav, German and Italian, Hindu and Chinaman, each brings his own peculiar customs and ideals. What a medley! And here on the American continent by the mingling of the peoples and under the stress of new conditions are being worked out hitherto unknown forms of social life.

Among Anglo-Saxon peoples the home has higherto been the centre of the life of the people. Burns' description of the Cotter's Saturday Night finds a response in every heart. We still have our home gatherings, but, as we have seen, many forces are at work in our great cities to lessen the predominating influence which was once exercised by the home. Even among the well-to-do the members of the family rarely spend an evening quietly together either alone or with a few friends. Every week brings numerous 'engagements' alike for parents and children, the church entertainment, the concert, or the theatre; the club, the lodge, the society, formal dinners and receptions – there are a hundred things that one cannot miss!

The workers are perhaps disposed to appreciate 'the fireside joys,' but alas, too often 'the home' is merely a sleeping-place. The man comes in tired and dirty; it is too much trouble to 'clean up.' The place is 'all of a litter,' for the wife too has been out working all day. The children are cross. They have had no well-cooked wholesome meal that day, or for many a day, and have been training one another all day. What wonder the man goes along to the corner to meet 'the boys' and spends the evening in the comfortable bar-room. The wife, poor woman, after her hard day's work – every day is with her washing-day or cleaning-day – has had to get supper for 'her man and the kids.' How can she have much energy to straighten up the house or entertain the children? Mary, who works in a laundry, hasn't to go back to-night to work, and so has arranged to go with some friends to the ten-cent theatre; don't be too hard on her. And Jack, oh, he was off with the gang before his father had finished supper. With slight variation, that picture is true of thousands of homes in our cities.

Among our newer arrivals are many who in the home lands have always sought their social life in public places. In a study of social conditions in Boston, the residents of the South End House tell of 'Life's Amenities' among the Italians (*Americans in Process*):

The lightheartedness of the Italians and their keen love of pleasure make an atmosphere so full of gaiety that a spectator for the time is led to overlook the many discomforts which must naturally fall to the share of a people so closely crowded together. But perhaps these discomforts affect the Italians less than any other race, for they love the open air and the general fellowship of their kind, and every possible moment is spent beyond the confines of the house walls. The first glimpse of spring brings with it thronging streets, crowded doorways and well-filled open windows; with uncovered heads, the women and girls saunter up and down the sidewalks, or with their bits of crocheted lace, intended for home decoration, sit in some doorway or at an open window, where they may gossip with a neighbor or join in a gay street song. Here too may be seen the curved knitting needle used by the older Italian woman as she rounds out the stocking for the coming winter. The men crowd the curbstone or open street, discussing the politics of their country, their personal injuries, or the possibilities for assisting some less fortunate brother. Groups of men and boys, numbering fifteen or twenty, congregate in some street or square, and immediately there is such emphatic utterance, fiery denunciation, violent gesture and all-pervading excitement as would convince the unaccustomed that a mass meeting was discussing the wrongs of a nation rather than that a casual group of neighbors were exchanging gossip ...

The loyalty of the Italian to the land of his birth, and his love of the dramatic, make him seek every opportunity for a folk festival. The anniversaries of the various benevolent and secret societies are often celebrated by processions of men and children carrying gay banners. These, together with the bright sashes of the little ones and the insignia worn by the men, cause one to feel that the Italians are truly a nation of children born to turn their world into a stage, with everyday life as the sufficient material of the play. Although they cannot be said to be a people of deep religious feeling, the historic associations of their Church and its unequalled pageantry appeal to their emotional natures.

The religion of the people always has its social side. Even in our Protestant churches, where ceremonial observances have a very small place, and which are individualistic rather than social in teaching and organization, there is increasing emphasis placed upon social life. 'Socials,' concerts, lectures, society meetings and 'institutional' features of all kinds are occupying a larger space on the programme of our churches' activity. Among the Roman Catholics and the Jews much of the social life centres about the great religious feasts and the special church observances connected with all the important events in life. In the chapter above quoted from *Americans in Process,* is the following concise description of one phase of Jewish life. It must be remembered that although the Jews are essentially a home-loving people, their conception of the family is broader than ours and retains many elements that are Patriarchal and Eastern in character.

The Jews have some social life in their various benevolent organiza-tions, culminating in an occasional dance; but their intensest interests of this sort centre about their many religious ceremonies. In every home the circumcising of the newly-born male child, the betrothal and the wedding of a son or daughter, are occasions of great moment, and are looked forward to as times of feasting and merry-making. The wedding is perhaps the most interesting of these three functions. The ceremony is rarely performed in the bride's home; the lavish hospitality of the occasion necessitating the hiring of some hall for the reception, even when the pair are married in the synagogue. The Oriental love for splendor and display is everywhere seen. Since it is possible to hire all things, even the wedding gown and veil, these are often, by the desire of the bride, mere temporary finery, in order that the money saved thereby may be used to increase the general gorgeousness of the occasion. The hospitality is unbounded. Not only are parents and brothers and sisters constantly

Glimpses of foreign life in our cities

Foreign 'stores' in Winnipeg
A friendly call
A book stand

on the alert to see that the guests are cared for, but the bride herself omits no effort for their comfort and enjoyment. Entire families are among the guests, from mothers with nursing babies to grandfathers and grandmothers, and all share the common joyousness.

At the ceremony, the father or mother of the bride accompanies her to the canopy, under which she stands facing the East. She is followed by an attendant who is the wife of the best man. The lights carried by the friends of the bride recall to memory the wise and foolish virgins of Holy Writ. The rabbi tells the pair that they take their vows as descendants of Abraham, Isaac and Jacob; gives them a dissertation on married life, and his blessing. After they have tasted the consecrated wine, the groom crushes the goblet under his heel to show to the world his determination to overcome all evil in the new life upon which they are entering. Dancing follows the ceremony, and lasts long into the night. Everybody tries to make everybody else happy. Young men and young women dance with small children as well as with each other, and pay an exquisite deference to their elders. The wedding supper is served at many tables so that all can sit down to the feast. The men often take their seats before the women, and always eat with their hats on.

One of our workers has contributed brief descriptions of a baptism, a wedding and a funeral, as she has seen them among our Slavic immigrants.

It is no unusual thing for a deaconess to be invited to attend the baptismal services of the new babes belonging to the women who attend mothers' meetings. These generally take place when the baby is about a week old, or on the second Sunday after its birth. The godparents, the father and the child generally go to the church for the service, and there is in many of the homes a baptismal feast afterwards. These feasts often end in fighting and police court cases. Among the Poles the glasses are filled with beer, and when they are emptied the guests deposit money in them for the baby. Several times our minister has been asked to baptize the children.

One of the most beautiful services I ever attended was one of this kind. The father came to our night-school and the mother to Mothers' Meeting. Shortly before the birth of the child the father, who had been out of work for months, secured a position in the country, but before leaving he called on the deaconess and asked her to be very good to his young wife, who was without friends here and who knew not a word of English. We cared for the mother, and after the birth of her child she asked that he be baptized in the little Mission that had thrown open its doors in welcome to strangers from a distant land and whose workers had so befriended them. The following Sunday evening a German neighbor and his wife brought the baby boy to our church. He wore a dainty white dress sent from the Mission and was wrapped in the long white veil worn by his mother on her wedding-day. The service was beautiful in its simplicity and yet most solemn, as the pastor explained the meaning of the baptismal vows to the God-parents of the child.

...

Her wedding-day is the most important day in the girl's life, and many are her plans to make it as happy and as long as possible. Her clothing is chosen, not with any thought of its usefulness or durability for the coming days, but only for the wedding-day. If it is soiled or torn during the festivities, what matters it? It was meant only for this occasion.

Most of the brides prefer to walk from their home to the church rather than have a cab, since it is less expensive, and more people can see their fine clothes. Many times the wedding guests form a procession headed by the contracting parties and walk the streets for several blocks, then go to a photographer's and have a picture taken.

To an outsider the service in the church is particularly interesting and impressive. Sometimes the parties go to the church before the wedding service for confession, but if the wedding is arranged for an early hour, as they so often are, confession and receiving the sacrament immediately precede the ceremony. Paid singers are usually engaged, and there is much singing and chanting. One part of the service is the placing of a crown of orange blossoms on the head of the bride and groom in turn. If this falls off, as it is quite possible it will, it is considered most unlucky, and the one from whose head it fell is supposed to have but a short time to live. Two wedding rings are used, so that both husband and wife have one.

Even during the service the bride's thoughts are too often on her dress instead of the solemn words that are being said, and if for a moment she seems to be entering into the service one of her bridesmaids will re-arrange her veil or pin on an extra flower so that she cannot long get away from the thought of her appearance.

After the service and walk the party adjourn to the home of the bride or to a hired hall, where the wedding-feast, consisting of many foreign dishes and much beer, is spread. After the meal is over, dancing begins. The table is shoved against the wall but is re-plenished from time to time, as additional guests are constantly coming, and all are at liberty to help themselves at any time. Beer, too, is there in unlimited quantities and is freely partaken of by both men and women. In a small house the air becomes stifling, but dancing continues far into the night or until next day. Many of the men become so drunk they can hardly stand and are often very quarrelsome. Everyone who dances with the bride is supposed to give her a present in money; this helps to 'set up' the young couple in house-keeping. The groom is supposed to pay for the cost of everything, and a Slavic wedding is generally an expensive affair, as open house must be kept.

As supplementing this description, we might note that the wedding of one of our Ruthenian girls, whose mother goes out washing, cost in the neighborhood of $150.00. The collection and presents amounted to $112.00. Out of this the young couple paid some of their expenses and bought a stove, a bed, and a dresser (used as a dresser and sideboard combined).

Some of the items of expenditure may be of interest. The bride's trousseau was in this case very simple — dress $8.00; veil $2.00; green sprays, $1.75; ribbon, $1.25; shoes, $2.50; underwear, $7.50. The bride also bought sheets, blankets and towels. The priest's fee was $5.50, candles, etc., extra; two singers, $1.50 each; orchestra, $12.00; rent of hall, $13.00; wine, $1.75 a bottle and beer, $3.00 a keg.

...

One of the saddest services I ever attended in a foreign home was the funeral of a little baby. The father was tubercular and had done no work for a considerable time. The mother was not very robust. The family had three beds in one room and made a little money by renting these at 5c. a space for a night.

When the baby died the city was asked to bear the expense of the funeral, but when the officer came to investigate he found a keg of beer just opened and several of the people none too sober. The city then asked the undertaker to collect the expenses from the family, saying, that if they could afford beer they could afford to pay.

Shortly before the hour of service a few of us went to the home. The room was as clean as hands could make it, and quite a number of people were sitting quietly waiting for the service to begin. At one end of the room was a table on which the dead child lay. Three beer bottles served as candle-holders at the head, and a large loaf of bread with a hole in the top served a similar purpose at the feet. The little form was clothed in white garments, and there was a great abundance of paper and wool flowers. The family were too poor to engage a priest, but a singer from their own church took charge of the service, which lasted for twenty minutes or half an hour. During the chanting the casket, table and dead child were sprinkled with holy water. At a sign from the singer the undertaker went to put the body into the casket, which he brought with him, but the mother interfered and would allow no hands but her own to touch her dead child. The grief of the parents was most touching, and our tears flowed freely.

But the saddest part was yet to come, for at the close of the service the undertaker had to tell the grief-stricken parents that he was instructed to collect the funeral expenses from them before removing the body. The parents explained that they had nothing with which to pay, and the neighbors and friends verified their statement and proved they had helped with the expense thus far, even to supplying the beer. The sobs of the mother were most heartbreaking, and finally the good-hearted undertaker took up the little casket, saying he would bear the expense himself if he could not collect it from the city, before he would cause that mother greater agony.

The cemetery was several miles distant, and as there was no way of taking the friends there, the undertaker promised to give them later the number of the grave so that they might visit it.

Another social worker in a personal letter has given me an account of a better class Polish wedding. Perhaps she will pardon my giving the letter a wider publicity than was intended.

Well, we have been to a Polish wedding — *bona fide* guests for whom the 'buggy,' a handsome cab and pair, called in due time. To be sure it was not in the body of the church, but in a chapel to the rear. Nevertheless the bride of fifteen in her white silk gown, with rose bouquet and long veil entwined with sprays of green, looked as bride-like as if she had not been working in a hotel up to the time of the marriage. The groom was a handsome fellow, just turned twenty, employed in one of the packing-houses of the city.

A great solemnity settled over the little chapel as in the dim light the young couple knelt before the alter. The priest went through a great deal of reading, manipulating the ring, handing lighted candles and censer-swinging before the 'sister,' and the choir boys, around the piano at the back, sang the final chant and the man and woman rose up, united for life.

Anon we found ourselves in a great hall some blocks distant. The tables ran along one side, leaving splendid accommodation for orchestra and dancers. Many of the latter were already tripping lightly over the floor, among them the fair little bride with her bridesmaid.

Throughout the evening the Canadian guests received the most gracious attention. They must be seated first and at the corner of the table beside the small and only stove in the hall; the members of the families concerned must greet them with pleasant smiles every time they passed; they must be given an opportunity to dance if they wished — in fact, many of the dances must be entered upon only after the guests had been introduced to them as from out the bygone days. Thank fortune, no one suspected the miserable forebodings lurking in the heart of at least one of these very guests, all smiling though she seemed; forebodings of what the later hours would bring — the hard drinking — for wine and beer there were in abundance; the unseemly familiarity; the brawling, ending in the inevitable fight to be settled only by police interference. But, do you know, none of it came, though we stayed until the bride's veil had been caught by a fair maiden with the same joy that one of our Canadian girls feels when she has wrested the bridal bouquet from all others.

Early in the evening came a light repast — cold meat, salads, bread, cake, fruit and liquors. At eleven o'clock, the wedding-feast proper was served — roast fowl, a Russian dish of rice rolled in a cabbage leaf and boiled, pears stewed and mixed with prunes, salads, cake of many varieties, fresh fruits — and always, always jugs of beer and bottles of wine. The refreshments were handled entirely by the

A Polish wedding group

immediate relatives of the groom, and though the mother's feet
persisted in wilfully keeping time to the pulsating music, and she did
find time to engage in a few of the time-honored dances, yet her
heart was ever upon hospitality intent and the smile with which she
served her guests was born of true womanly gladness in ministering
to the pleasure of her friends.

Throughout the evening the orchestra played with only the
briefest of intermissions and, repast or no repast, the dancing never
ceased. And what dances they were − the ever-graceful waltz, then a
two-step or a polka, something at all events 'not Polish' (with a
shrug) but 'English' and engaged in by only the younger people.
There was a Cossack dance, in which at times each man almost seated
himself upon the floor. This was followed by a lengthy folk-dance, a
gladsome thing for which, at the start, all had to line up in couples.
Finally came the Polonaise, I think they called it. I was chatting with
the Patriarch of the evening when his eye suddenly brightened as he
observed this time had come. 'Sie suchen Geld,' said he, and led me
into the great circle. We stood there while each gentleman in turn
danced with the bride, and then dropped his contribution into the
lap of the girl-friend seated within the circle, and the wedding
celebration was at an end.

The whole evening had been a revelation to us. We had watched a
zealous young Polish-Canadian working strenuously to preserve
something of their national pleasures to his people, and we respected
him. We had seen his brother guarding among them the spirit of
music and song, and we admired him. At the close of the feast we
had listened to the 'Declamation' by the Patriarch to the young
couple − 'Life is not all music and dancing; there will be the dark
side too; there must be toil and weariness, but be true to the best of
the Old Land and the New. If children are granted you, shield them,
be patient with them, teach them, that they may be a helpful
example to others.' We had listened to the Patriarch, I say, and we
honored him.

And as in the early morning hours, tired and chilly, we turned our
steps homeward, my comrade and I smiled in each other's faces in
the joy of a new, great, glad hope for the future of our Polish-
Canadians.

Among the foreign immigrants there are many societies and clubs,
some national, some political, some educational or social. These

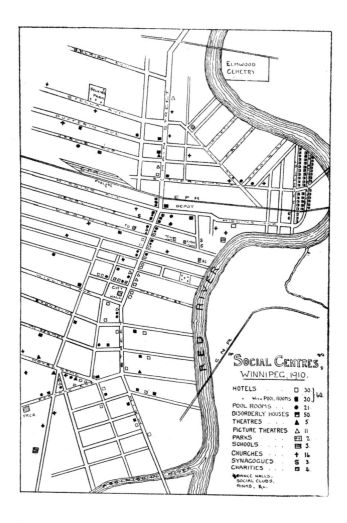

Down-town section of Winnipeg, showing centres of social life

frequently give concerts, theatricals and dances and play quite an important part in the life of the foreign community.

Apart from the facilities provided by such private organizations, where may the public generally find their social life, amusement and recreation? In the hotel, the theatre, the pool-room and the dance hall. Perhaps our parks in summer and the skating rinks in winter ought to be included in the list. Our church people have often assumed an attitude of uncompromising hostility to all such resorts, but what have they provided in their place? The church activities, the Y.M.C.A. and the Y.W.C.A. provide for the social needs of only a very limited class and that class probably not the most needy. Where are the mass of the people to spend their hours of leisure? It is not the place here to point out the evils of intemperance, gambling and immorality so often associated with the saloon, the pool-room and the public dance hall, but we do assert strongly that a merely repressive policy is altogether inadequate to meet the situation. The need for recreation and amusement is a natural one and must be supplied in some innocent and legitimate manner, or it will seek satisfaction in ways that are abnormal and demoralizing. We must remember, too, that many of our newer citizens bring with them drinking customs and folk dances that are treasured as an integral part of their social and national inheritance. These cannot be immediately done away with by unsympathetic, if zealous, reformers, who have entirely different standards. Indeed, under proper safeguards many customs which at first glance might be condemned may be found to be a valuable addition to the variety and richness of our social life. The Maypole is again being erected in Merrie England, and in the United States historic pageants with their folk-songs and dances are beginning to possess no small educational value.

One of the more recent forms of amusement calls for special mention — the moving-picture show. The rapid spread of this type of theatre is most remarkable. A whole group of constantly expanding business interests centre about the new and popular attraction. Someone has said that it is the most powerful single social force in America. It has been denounced as utterly bad, and yet the saloon people state that it is cutting down their profits, as people find it cheaper and pleasanter to sit in the theatre than in the bar-room. The fact is, that in itself the picture business is neither good nor bad. All depends upon the character of the pictures. Some of these are abominably vile and foster crime and immorality of all kinds. The majority are simply cheap and vulgar or silly. A few provide excellent entertainment and instruction. Improvement may be made along two lines. First every city or community ought to maintain a strict censorship by which all immoral or debasing pictures could be absolutely prohibited; this is now being done in many cities and is not so difficult to carry out as might be supposed. In the second place there ought to be a campaign of education through which the public would gradually come to appreciate and demand a higher grade of pictures. There is no reason why the picture show should not become of great educational value. The trouble is that in all such matters attempted reform has rarely been along constructive lines.

In many of the American cities the Public School buildings are being utilized as social centres. This is a move in the right direction and should be copied in Canada. In the country, 'the little red schoolhouse' was a real social centre. Concerts, lectures, tea-meetings, all were held there as a matter of course. Political meetings, meetings to consider any public interest, were called at the school. In many cases, the various religious bodies in the earlier days held services in the schoolhouse on alternate Sundays. Why should not the city school perform some such useful functions for the city? The expensive school plant is used only for five or six hours, five days in the week and nine months in the year. Why not run it full time? In the basement could be a gymnasium and baths, in the class rooms all sorts of classes and clubs, in the assembly halls concerts and public meetings. Especially where there is a cosmopolitan population do we need a common meeting-place.

From an article in *The Survey* on the 'Rochester Social Centres' we clip the following:

The real place of the social centre in the community life is expressed in this song whose form is doggerel, but which is nevertheless popular because it is true:

THE SOCIAL CENTRE
Air: Mr. Dooley.
'There are several parties here in our communitee,
Republican and Democrat and Socialist – that's three;
They never get together just because they disagree;
But there's a place where all of them can talk things over free.

Chorus — 'It's-at-the-centre,
   The social centre,
   The place where everybody feels at home;
   Forgets th' external,
   And gets fraternal;
   There's something doing there — you'd better come.

'There are many churches here in our communitee;
Some of them are better and all of them are good.
But Catholic and Protestant and Jew are kept apart,
There's just one place where we all know that we are one at heart.

'There are a lot of races here in our communitee;
English, French, Italian, Greek, Dane, Swede, Hindoo, Chinee;
And sometimes they forget that we are all one familee;
But there's a place where this is just the fact that you will see.

'Now there are some distinctions that are seen upon the street,
For some folks ride in auto cars and some ride on their feet,
And worry about the price of clothes comes in and spoils the fun,
But there's a place where hats are off, and rich and poor are one.

'There are little social circles here, each with its coterie;
Some in saloons, some pedro cliques, some soaking up pink tea,
But everyone is glad there is a place where each one gets
A chance to be acquainted with the folks in other sets.'

In a chapter on the 'Control of Leisure,' Wilcox writes in *The American City*:

Our programme for the checking of vice and the building up of the best type of democratic citizenship should include:
   1 All kinds of helpful social activity that will tend to increase the usefulness of the school and the school building as a social centre.
   2 The performance on the part of the city of all the public functions which the saloon has now appropriated to itself, such as the supply of safe and attractive drinking water, the supply of toilet conveniences, and the provision of a place where social life may centre without the dollar mark on it.

3 The provision of accessible public parks, athletic fields, gymnasia, public baths and other means of physical activity for health and recreation.

4 The active cultivation of municipal art by the suppression of nuisances, such as unsightly poles, flaming billboards, repulsive advertisements and the contamination of the air with smoke and dust; by the construction of beautiful public buildings, and the adornment of the streets and other public places; and, in the great cities, by the establishment of art galleries, museums and municipal theatres.

5 The encouragement of civic devotion through the use of municipal ceremonials, the attractive report to the citizens of official action, and especially the *bona fide* effort to serve the interests of the people so that they will love and respect their government rather than distrust and despise it.

6 Most important of all, the cultivation by all possible means, public as well as private, of the ideal of civic righteousness as the only safe basis of freedom and the only legitimate source of civic pride.

REFERENCES

'Youth: Its Education, Regimen and Hygiene'
G. Stanley Hall. New York: D. Appleton & Co.
'The Boy Problem'
W. B. Forbush. Boston: The Pilgrim Press
'Constructive and Preventive Philanthropy'
Joseph Lee. New York: The Macmillan Co.
'Substitutes for the Saloon'
Raymond Calkins. Boston: Houghton, Mifflin Co.
'The Wider Use of the School Plant'
Clarence Arthur Perry. New York: Charities Publication Committee
'The Immigrant Tide'
Edward A. Steiner. Fleming H. Revell
'The Italian in America'
Lord, Trenor and Barrows. New York: B. F. Buck & Co.
'The Russian Jew in the United States'
Chas. S. Bernheimer. Philadelphia: John C. Winston Co.

'Our Slavic Fellow Citizens'
Emily Greene Balch. New York: Charities Publication Committee
'Little Aliens'
Myra Kelly. New York: Charles Scribner's Sons
'The Melting Pot'
Israel Zangwill.

Chapter 6

Religious tendencies

The city is the challenge to the Church to-day, and we have a generation instead of a century in which to meet it.

Josiah Strong

The city is from one-half to one-quarter as well supplied with
churches as the whole country; and moreover, the church, like the
home, grows weaker as the city grows larger.

Strong

To make cities — that is what we are here for. To make good
cities — that is for the present hour the main work of Christianity.
For the city is strategic. It makes the towns; the towns make the
villages; the villages make the country. He who makes the city makes
the world.

Henry Drummond

The problem of how to save the slums is no more difficult than the
problem of how to save the people who have moved away from
them and are living in the suburbs, indifferent to the woes of their
fellow mortals. The world can be saved if the Church does not save
it. The question is, can the Church be saved unless it is doing all in its
power to save the world?

Graham Taylor

IN A series of rather startling articles published in the *American Magazine* in 1909, Ray Stannard Baker gives the results of his study of the religious conditions in New York City. I cannot better introduce our subject than by quoting from one of his articles. As we read, let us ask ourselves if we can perceive any similar tendencies in our own cities.

The church workers themselves feel that the churches are somehow inadequate to their great task of spiritual leadership. Something is felt to be wanting.

The Reverend Charles E. Jefferson of the Broadway Tabernacle, the oldest and one of the largest Congregational churches in the city, said last year in a sermon; 'While the Church has been filled with doubts and fears, there has been an ever deepening estrangement between the Church and large classes of population ... The last decade has been the most strenuous and discouraging for Christian workers which this city has probably ever known.'

Not long before his resignation, broken down with over-work, Dr. Rainsford of St. George's Episcopal Church struck the same note of despondency — calling attention to the falling away in the size of the Sunday congregations in spite of the most strenuous activities to keep the work at white heat. The late Reverend George C. Lorimer of the Madison Avenue Baptist Church said in one of his last sermons: 'There is such a thing as a religious crisis in America, however much we may scoff at the idea. Religion is to-day of very low vitality.'

Many other New York ministers have made statements of similar tenor, which are indeed substantiated more or less definitely by the findings of the Reverend Dr. Walter Laidlaw of the Federation of Churches, who has made extensive sociological and statistical studies of Church conditions in New York city. Dr. Laidlaw estimated that in 1905 there were over one million (1,071,981) churchless Protestants in the city. By churchless Protestants are meant people whose antecedents were Protestant, and who, if they became interested in religious work, would naturally associate themselves with some Protestant church. Dr. Laidlaw shows, moreover, that the membership in Protestant churches, in spite of rapidly increasing population, has barely held its own in Greater New York, while on Manhattan Island there has been an actual loss of membership ...

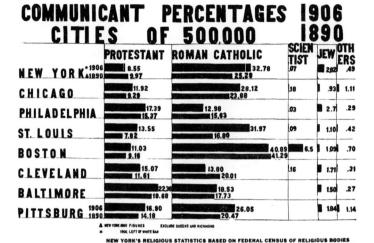

COMMUNICANT PERCENTAGES 1906
CITIES OF 500,000   1890

	PROTESTANT	ROMAN CATHOLIC	SCIEN TIST	JEW	OTH ERS
NEW YORK *1906	8.55	32.78	.07	2.82	.49
▲1890	9.97	25.29			
CHICAGO	11.92	28.12	.18	.93	1.11
	9.29	23.88			
PHILADELPHIA	17.39	12.98	.03	2.7	.29
	15.37	15.63			
ST. LOUIS	13.55	31.97	.09	1.10	.42
	7.82	16.80			
BOSTON	11.03	40.89	6.5	1.99	.70
	9.16	41.29			
CLEVELAND	15.07	13.80	.16	1.71	.31
	11.61	20.01			
BALTIMORE	22.36	18.53		1.50	.27
	19.68	17.73			
PITTSBURG 1906	16.90	26.05		1.84	1.14
1890	14.18	20.47			

▲ NEW YORK 1890 FIGURES   EXCLUDE QUEENS AND RICHMOND
■   1906, LEFT OF WHITE BAR

NEW YORK'S RELIGIOUS STATISTICS BASED ON FEDERAL CENSUS OF RELIGIOUS BODIES

	POPULATION	Protestant Communicants	Roman Catholic	Other Catholic	Jewish Synagogues	Other Religions	Scientist	TOTALS
Dec 31 1906	4,312,570	369,318	1 413,775	18,067	*39,414	3,536	3,372	1,838,482
June 1 1890	2 507 414	261 786	621 815	1 226	*38,155	6,572	420	929,974

* Heads of families with Synagogue connection, multiplied by 4. in computing percentage

Statistics showing religious tendencies of the largest cities of the United States

The Roman Catholic Church has felt a similar loss of power; not only in New York, but in other great American cities. Concerning this tendency we have the word of no less a personage than Archbishop Falconio, apostolic delegate from the Pope, spoken at the first great missionary conference of the Roman Catholic Church in America, held last spring in Chicago. He said:

'In our day a spirit of religious indifferentism and relaxation of Christian morality is permeating the sanctuary of Christian families. To check this dangerous tendency we need a revival of the true Christian spirit. Besides, in some dioceses numerous Catholics are in want of priests, churches and schools; there are immigrants who are in need of religious assistance.'

And the Roman Catholic is not more concerned than the Jew. Although the Jewish population of New York City is growing rapidly, the same disheartenment exists among Jewish religious leaders as among Christians. The Jews, especially of the younger generation, show a growing inclination to drift away from the synagogues and the teachings of the fathers.

A close observer, the Reverend Charles Stelzle, Superintendent of the Labor Department of the Presbyterian Church, who sees the church from the point of view of the working-man, says:

'The Church to-day seems to have arrived at one of the most crucial periods of her history ... No one can successfully deny that the Church is slowly but surely losing ground in the city. Nearly every city in America is witnessing the removal of its churches from the densely populated sections where the church is most needed. Within recent years forty Protestant churches moved out of the district below Twentieth Street in New York City, while 300,000 people moved in. Alarmed for her safety and her very life, the Church has sounded a dismal retreat in the face of the greatest opportunity which has ever come to her!

'Not only have the working classes become alienated from the churches, especially from the Protestant churches, but a very large proportion of well-to-do men and women who belong to the so-called cultured class, have lost touch with church work. Some retain membership, but the church plays no vital or important part in their lives. Thousands of men and women contribute to the support of the churches, yet allow no church duty to interfere with the work or pleasures of their daily lives. They are neither inspired nor commanded.'

It is easy to say that this article is pessimistic; that its statements are exaggerated and inferences unwarranted; but the fact nevertheless remains that many religious leaders are convinced that the Church, as an organization, does not exercise the predominating influence in the lives of its members that once it did, and that it is not to-day coping successfully with the great social problems which, in their acutest form, are found in the city. It is well that our churches in Canada should pause and reflect and if possible check the dangerous tendencies which we must admit are already in evidence among us.

Many of us personally have experienced the transition from country to city life. May not a study of our own varied adventures and the changes in our own own conceptions and manner of life suggest the reasons for the transformation that is taking place in the religious life of to-day? Further, we may thus perceive some of its dangers and its possibilities. Let me give a somewhat typical case. Dave Burke was, as he would put it, 'raised' in the country. The home life was wholesome. He had received a fair education at 'the little red schoolhouse.' The social life centred very largely about the church at the 'Corners.' Here every week he attended church and Sunday school. Here he met the neighbors and his own particular friends. Here were held the tea meetings and lectures and socials and concerts. Every winter there used to be revival meetings that for weeks were the dominating influence in the community. Dave could just remember these. As he grew into young manhood there were being introduced Conventions and Epworth Leagues and Institutes, and later Summer Schools. The minister was a frequent visitor at the Burke home, and indeed he was regarded as being as essential to the life of the community as was the King to the existence of the Empire.

Unexpected changes came in the Burke household and Dave decided to try his luck in the city. After a few days' search he stumbled on a job in the shipping department of a wholesale house. His muscle and general hardiness were the only things he had to fall back on now. A chance acquaintance had directed him to a cheap boarding-house. He found himself in an absolutely different world; how different some of us can easily imagine from our own experience.

And the church! The first Sunday his room-mate — for of course he had to 'double-up' — 'lay in' and breakfast was late — and the morning was gone. In the afternoon, he took a walk about the city. The Salvation Army band attracted him and he went into the barracks — then out again on the street. He was miserably lonely — nothing to do — no place to go — no one he knew. At night he went with one of the boys to a large church. It was grand. He had never seen such a crowd, and the organ — it almost frightened him when they let it loose. But the minister and the choir all seemed so far away. As he went out, a well-dressed young fellow shook hands with him and, shoving a card into his hand, asked him to come to the League on Monday. Dave, hungry for companionship, next evening summoned up his courage and after circling the church twice sneaked into a back seat. But he was not comfortable. These city folks seemed so different that he was glad to get out without anyone having spoken to him.

Five years have passed. Dave has seen and learned much. He has now a somewhat better position and a more comfortable boarding-place. Occasionally he goes to church — he says he likes the music. Often he stays at home and reads a magazine. 'Home' he calls it. It's not likely he will ever have a home of his own now. No, he hasn't formed any bad habits. The old life is still potent. But it is the old life — that is the pity of it. The country church ministered to his higher needs, the city church has somehow failed.

In studying the religious problem of the city we may roughly divide the city into three parts: (1) The 'good residential' districts; (2) the down-town districts; (3) the poorer districts. In the good residential districts live our well-to-do Canadian people, mostly of the business or professional classes. Our cities have been growing so rapidly that many of these people have at first lived in town, then moved out to better homes in the suburbs. In these districts there are many churches. It is the respectable thing to attend church and the people are eminently respectable and traditions are strong. Faithful pastors are doing good work and the possibilities are great. Will the church continue to hold this class? In many of the American cities that have developed a little beyond our present stage the Church is losing its hold. The wealthier classes have grown away from it. The middle classes are still attached to the church but their children have many new interests and the church no longer exercises a vital and dominating influence in their lives. Perhaps its programme is too limited!

Second, we have the down-town districts. These were, in the earlier days, the residential districts, but business has expanded and crowded out the homes. But people still are here – living in hotels and blocks, in apartments and boarding-houses – more people than occupied the same area when it was a region of homes. What of the religious life of the down-town districts? In our own cities we still have splendid down-town churches. But already the church members who have moved to the suburbs are selling the old churches and re-building in more convenient localities. In fact, the property is too valuable to be kept for a church; it must be sold in order that on it may be erected a theatre or a departmental store!

Yet the district swarms with people – the very people who most need those ministrations which the church exists to supply. Again let us endeavor to look ahead a few years. Shall we abandon the field? This is the line of least resistance and the one usually followed. Many plausible arguments are advanced. The people who purchased the site and erected the building may surely sell again and rebuild the church in the neighborhood where they now live. And then a portion of the money realized could be used to assist the enterprises of the church! So perhaps a 'Mission' is established and a minister and a deaconess engaged to preach the gospel and dole out old clothes and Christmas treats. Or the church, realizing its larger obligations, resolves to 'stay with the job' and adapt itself to the needs of its changed constituency. Then follows probably the development of institutional features through which an attempt is made to minister to the various physical, educational and social requirements of the down-town classes.

As one studies the situation in the American cities he is impressed with the fact that the churches have not solved the down-town problem – they are only beginning to realize it. We in Canada are just entering upon this new stage in our development. As we see moving-picture shows and vaudeville performances presented in buildings consecrated by our fathers to the worship of God – buildings which have through the years witnessed spiritual struggles and triumphs, buildings from which have gone forth those mighty moral forces that have established our present civilization – as we see such changes can we but ask 'What of the future?'

Leaving the down-town districts, we come to the third and most complex division of the city – the poorer sections. The poor we have always had. But until recent years they were small in number, of our own speech and blood, and not segregated in distinct quarters. But with the growth of our cities, the influx of foreign immigrants, and the development of our industrial life we have now large areas known as undesirable residential districts – in some instances bad enough to be called slums. Here we find the waste of society – those who have not 'made good,' the unfortunate, the depraved. Here are those who have had to remain at the bottom – the unskilled workers of all kinds. Here too settle, at first, the newcomers who must start at the bottom. And so to complicate an already difficult problem we have our 'foreign colonies' – our Ghettos, Little Italys, Colored Blocks and Chinatowns, and whole foreign wards with their mixed population from Southeastern Europe.

What of the religious life of these communities? In districts which had formerly been occupied by English-speaking people, the Protestant churches persist for some time. But as their constituency gradually decreases, some withdraw; others, financially embarrassed – without workers living in the vicinity, without adequate outside support – continue to fight a losing battle. Here, as in the downtown districts, a few churches are endeavoring to meet the new conditions. Missions are established; deaconesses employed; foreign-speaking agents secured, when possible, and charitable work organized. But so far these efforts have been hopelessly inadequate.

Again looking to the American cities, we find that Social Settlements and Charity Organization Societies have done the most efficient work in such districts. Church missions, although often doing good work in a limited way, cannot be said to have been very successful. In the English cities the great City Missions have done splendid work, but it must be borne in mind that they are working largely among a homogeneous people, with a common language and with Protestant and British traditions.

The non-English peoples who come to us bring their religions with them. A study of their beliefs, organizations and customs cannot be attempted here; and yet it should be borne in mind that until we do really understand the religions of these peoples we can hardly hope to influence them greatly.

In a general way we may divide our foreign churches into Protestant, Catholic and Jewish.

In down-town Toronto

Once a church, now a theatre
The church lost in the shadow of the factory

The Lutheran Church has a large following among the Germans and Scandinavians. There are also the Reformed Church, the Baptist, Mennonite, Mission Friends and various other smaller bodies. The home tongue often binds the immigrants closely to one another and to the church in which are conserved many of the associations of the home land. But as the young people learn and use the English language and mingle with English people, there is a tendency to break away from the church with the foreign language and customs. Some of these churches in order to hold their young people are modernizing their forms and using English for at least one Sunday service. They are thus gradually entering on the same stage as the other Protestant churches that were established earlier in this country.

The Catholic Church might be considered essentially one — it is in type, and yet we have Roman, Greek, Syrian, Independent and National Catholic churches and Uniat churches. Then the strictly Catholic Church of Rome is divided as it works among the peoples of various nationalities and languages, as German and French and Polish and Italian Catholic. Thus it is simply impossible to make accurate generalizations in regard to the work of the 'Catholic Church.' Subject to many qualifications and exceptions and explanations perhaps we might venture the following: The Church has a strong hold on the immigrant peoples as they arrive in this country. They fear it and they love it. Its power has been almost absolute in the lands from which they come. It, more than anything else, unites them with the old land and all that they once held dear. The church is a home, a meeting-place, an entrance into the larger world of music and art and emotion.

But as time goes on better education and frequent intercourse with English-speaking Protestants and the prevailing spirit of the new world tend inevitably to weaken the power of the church. The men especially refuse to be guided by those whom they regard as their exploiters. In their revolt against the church they are called and call themselves Atheists and Socialists — which simply means that they are against the established order as they know it. Yet, they often maintain an outward adherence to the church as through its schools and societies are perpetuated their native language and national customs, and its services are required by custom in all the important events of their lives. The men might break with custom, but not the women – especially when the custom is associated with a pageant. Thus the church often retains its hold upon the people long after it has ceased to nourish them.

In all our larger cities we have large numbers of Jewish people. As soon as the community grows to any size a synagogue is established. This is the general meeting-place of the people. The old people attend with great regularity and the younger men generally observe to a greater or less degree the great religious festivals. But if one can separate the two ideas, it is nationality rather than religion that binds the younger generations to the synagogues. When the persecution which has intensified national feeling is at an end it is a question as to how long the Jews will remain a 'peculiar people.' It has been said that the younger generation of Jews on this continent are without a religion. That is too sweeping a statement, but certainly their moral, social, and spiritual conceptions are undergoing a vast change. The young people are cutting loose from the old moorings and venturing forth on unknown seas. A high idealism, sordid materialism, educational ambitions, vulgar vanity, socialistic tendencies, an intense nationalism – such are the various currents and winds that are driving them hither and thither, into what final harbor who can tell?

In face of such conditions our Protestant churches may well consider carefully their duties and responsibilities, their ideals and methods of work. What ought to be the attitude of the Protestant churches to the Catholic churches and to the Jewish synagogues? Then another and a very different question: How can Protestant Canadians best help their Catholic and Jewish neighbors? They have become a part of our community; we cannot ignore their presence; we cannot be indifferent to their welfare. Here we encounter one of the most serious problems that has ever faced our Canadian people. The Protestant Church, as has been said, is on its trial.

Another equally serious question is the attitude of the Church toward the workers. Shailer Mathews in *The Church and the Changing Order* writes:

The Protestant Churches are composed almost exclusively of those who belong to, or who are in sympathy with, the capitalistic classes – employers, salaried persons, farmers, and those engaged in personal service of such persons, like cooks, housemaids and coachmen. This fact and the far more discreditable one that church members have been too often notoriously indifferent to the need of applying the principles they profess to believe to industrial matters, have led the wage-earning class as a whole to regard the Church as an institution allied with capitalism and the local church as a social club.

In the meantime, the church seems happy in its lot. Here and there, it is true, there is some effort made at conciliation; but in general the church seems ready to rest under the onus of the accusation of being a class organization, and the clergy seem too often indifferent to the fact that they are hardly more than co-operatively sustained private chaplains of well-to-do cliques.

Dr. Richard T. Ely in *Social Aspects of Christianity* says:

The Church has in recent years for the most part contented herself with repeating platitudes and vague generalities, which have disturbed no guilty soul, and thus she has allowed the leadership in social science to slip away from her. It can, then, scarcely excite surprise that communism has become infidel and socialism materialistic. Has she not, indeed, without any careful examination of their claims, hastened to condemn them to please the rich? ... First, these church leaders are so far away from the toiling masses that they fail to understand their desires and the motives of their actions. Second, the failure to rebuke wickedness in high places is noticed. Third, the negative attitude of the church with respect to every proposed reform discourages, disgusts, and even angers, working-men.

We must not shut our eyes. How far are these things true? Has the church been able to apply its teachings, to adapt its ritual and to modernize its machinery to meet the needs of existing social conditions?

Compare the scope of the Church's activity in mediæval times with that in our own. Medical knowledge was largely confined to the monasteries. The light of education, though it burned low, was kept alive in the cloister. Literature, limited as it was, nevertheless came from the schools and universities established by the Church. The law was more or less in the hands of the clergy. Charity was dispensed by the Church. Government was maintained and kings reigned because of the support of ecclesiastical authorities.

In the heart of the city loomed the great cathedral, the meeting-place of the people, the social and commercial and political centre of the city. In short, the church as an organization dominated the whole life of the people. Gradually the church has ceased to perform many of the functions that were once exclusively hers. An archbishop may assist at a coronation or a chaplain open the Legislature with prayer, but government no longer depends upon the sanction of the Church. Education, literature, music, art, law, medicine, all have burst from ecclesiastical control and pursue their way more or less independently. Modern Science and Industry were born free. Even Charity, which has been more or less under Church patronage, is attaining maturity and will soon leave her mother's home to establish one of her own. In the great cities we have seen the little old-fashioned church overgrown with ivy dwarfed into insignificance by the skyscrapers that surround it. Business has encroached on every side till little remains even of the graveyard — below which, in fact, runs the underground electric. It is a relic of the past, not a vital force in the life of the community.

Should we mourn that the Church is losing ground or rejoice that her life is now pulsating in a hundred new organizations? Is the Church's mission accomplished or is she but entering into a realization of the greatness and glory of her work?

> The old order changeth, yielding place to new,
> And God fulfils Himself in many ways,
> Lest one good custom should corrupt the world.
> Comfort thyself.

Every Methodist should be proud of the advanced ground taken by our last General Conference. In the report of the Committee on the State of the Work, we find the following:

Each age of the Church would seem to have its specific task; that of our own age the Christian Church is coming to recognize as the establishment of the Kingdom of God on the earth. The new conception of the missionary enterprise as not only the salvation of individuals but the uplifting and redemption of nations and races, with the new enthusiasm begotten of it as illustrated in the Student

Volunteer and Laymen's Missionary Movements; the ever mightier
and more varied and scientific philanthropies; the growing passion
for clean and beautiful and well ordered cities; the awakening to the
recognition that that land is doomed in which righteousness is not
public and national as well as private and personal — all these indicate what as yet the Church only partially realizes, that a definitely
new chapter in Christian history has been begun, and that the
Christian life of to-day cannot justly be measured by the standards
of the past. There is to-day a Christianity without the Church which
the Church fails to recognize only with loss and discouragement, and
a Christianity within the Church which finds its expression in service
rather than conventional religious exercises; and the most efficient
church will be the church which guides its membership most
generally and heartily into the widest variety of human service.

This report and the report of the Committee on Sociological
Questions should be read by all. They are authority for and pro-
phecy of a new programme for our churches.

REFERENCES

Social Aspects of Religion — See References Ch. I
Reports of Church bodies, Missionary Societies, City Missions
Current magazine articles
Reports — Social Settlements
Make a map of your city, showing location of churches
Make a map of your city, showing location of hotels, theatres, pool-
rooms and dance-halls
Interview representative business men
Attend workingmen's meeting
Take a walk during the time of Sunday evening service
Visit the slum district
Try to start a reform

Chapter 7

City government

In the country, though a man's life and property may be in greater danger than in the city, still safety generally depends upon the man *himself* ... while in the city a man's life and property are being continuously put in the hands of the community at large.

Wilcox in The American City

The city is indeed the visible symbol of the annihilation of distance and the multiplication of interests – and yet, on the other hand, the city emphasizes locality and gives opportunity for co-operation.

Wilcox

The hindrances to good citizenship – they are indolence, personal self-interest, party spirit.

James Bryce

Christian individuals should strengthen and protect the communistic institutions already in existence in society and help them to extend their functions.

Rauschenbusch

A starved dog at the city's gate
Foretells the ruin of the State.

Blake

'THE ANNUAL expenditure of Winnipeg already exceeds that of Manitoba; Montreal that of the Province of Quebec; and until the present year Toronto that of the Province of Ontario ... Speaking generally of the larger towns and cities, the present (1907) shows municipal operations of growing magnitude in the hands of men who have not been entrusted with similar responsibilities in any other field.' Wickett, *University of Toronto Studies.*

Immense responsibilities in the hands of unskilled and untried men – powerful private interests – a rapidly increasing purchasable vote – a largely indifferent public; there you have a situation serious enough to call for the most earnest consideration of every good citizen.

Yet it is probably safe to say that not one man in a thousand can give anything like a clear account of the machinery and functions of the government of his own city. Perhaps we might venture further, that not one in ten thousand is prepared to write a thesis dealing with the general problem. When the 'Civic Revival' reaches Canada it is to be hoped that not only will general interest be quickened, but that at least a few of our strongest men will devote themselves to this neglected field. The whole question of City Government is very complicated. Its history is involved, its details intricate, its ramifications almost interminable, its variations innumerable, and, more confusing than all, new and unexpected developments are taking place almost daily. All of which doubtless means simply that it is a 'live question.' Our brief treatment can at best be only, as it were, a peep through a window. Perhaps a few may be sufficiently interested to enter and inspect the house for themselves.

Politically or legally the city is subordinate to the state – that is, it derives its powers from and is responsible to the state. In determining the sphere of municipal action two general methods have been adopted. I quote from Goodnow (*City Government in the United States*):

One, that adopted by England and the United States, starts from the point of view of the state and lays down the rule that the city may not act except where it has been authorized expressly and specifically by the state. This view of the city's position has led to the practice of enumerating in detail its powers, particularly its financial powers, and to the adoption by the courts of the rule of strict

construction of all grants of power to cities ... The other method of
determining the competence of the city is the one adopted generally
on the Continent. It starts from the point of view of the city, and
adopts the principle that the presumption is always in favor of the
city, which has power to do anything which it has not been forbidden to do or which has not been entrusted to some governmental
authority other than the municipality. This theory of the position of
the city is based upon the conception that the city has a life separate
and apart from that of the state as a whole.

The situation in Canada is thus stated by Mr. Wickett: 'Municipal
powers in Canada are at present enumerated in as great detail as in
the United States, in much greater detail than in England, where an
efficient local government board exists, and in still greater detail
than on the continent of Europe, where administrative supervision is
carried further than in Great Britain. The result in this country is
frequent appeals to the Legislature for fragmentary additional
powers and in the interim serious delays and interruptions to municipal business.' And elsewhere he states: 'The further effect is
frequently felt of such a policy introducing party politics or inter-
municipal "log-rolling" into local issues.' It should be added that in
the newer Western cities incorporation is being granted on more
general terms.

In the charter obtained by Montreal in 1899 general powers were
granted, though the subsequent enumeration suggests limitations. As
this document gives a good idea of the scope of municipal activities
we quote at length:

It shall be lawful for the city council to enact, repeal or amend and
enforce by-laws for the peace, order, good government and general
welfare of the city of Montreal, and for all matters and things what-
soever that concern and affect the city of Montreal as a city and
body public and corporate, provided always that such by-laws be not
repugnant to the laws of this province or of Canada, nor contrary to
any special provisions of this charter.

And for the greater certainty, but not so as to restrict the scope
of the foregoing provision or of any power otherwise conferred by
this charter, nor to exceed the proviso herein above mentioned, it is
hereby declared that the authority and jurisdiction of the said city

council extends and shall hereafter extend to all matters coming within and affecting or affected by the classes of subjects next hereinafter mentioned, that is to say: 1. The raising of money by taxation; 2. The borrowing of money on the city's credit; 3. Streets, lanes, and highways, and the rights of passage above, across, or beneath the same; 4. Sewers, drains and aqueducts; 5. Parks, squares and ferries; 6. License for trading and peddling; 7. The public peace and safety; 8. Health and sanitation; 9. Vaccination and inoculation; 10. Public works and improvements; 11. Explosive substances; 12. Nuisances; 13. Markets and abattoirs; 14. Decency and good morals; 15. Masters and servants; 16. Water, light, heat, electricity and railways; 17. The granting of franchises and privileges to persons or companies; 18. The inspection of food.

In this determination of the relative powers of city and state, two tendencies rather opposite in direction are observable in the United States and Canada. The first is the demand for a larger measure of home-rule by the cities. This is prompted in part by the feeling that the business of the city belongs essentially to the city and should not be hampered by outside interference or refusals to grant authority. In part it is the revolt against the domination of corrupt machine politics, through which valuable city franchises have been secured by greedy corporations.

The second tendency is the extension of administrative supervision by the Government. It is felt that the state is virtually concerned in the welfare of the city, and that, free from local influence, it may exercise a most beneficial control. Thus, we have for example our Provincial Board of Health and Federal Railway Commission.

Coming to the machinery of city government we find great differences in our various cities. In a general way, it may be said that the British type is fundamental, that the American modifications of this type have had a decided influence, and that these with local adaptations have created an almost new system — if such the rather complex resultant may be called.

In the simple English type the people elect a council which in turn appoints its mayor, its committees and executive officers. In the United States, the city government was early modified along the lines of the state constitution. The mayor was elected by the people.

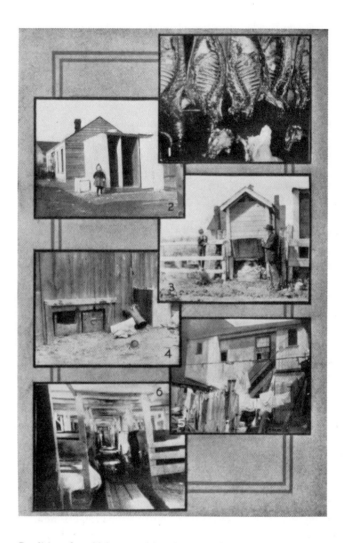

Conditions for which every citizen is responsible

1 Diseased meat, seized by Health Department
2, 3, 4 Horribly unsanitary conditions existing in some sections of our cities
5 A back yard – this stairway is the only entrance to one home
6 A stable producing conditions illustrated in no 1

The council was divided into two chambers, legislative and administrative. For a time much of the business was carried on by boards,
often appointed by the Legislature and largely independent of the
council. In recent years there has been a disposition to make the
mayor the responsible official with large powers.

In Canada, as in the United States, the mayor is elected. The
municipal offices are filled by the mayor and council. The separation
of the legislative and administrative functions is being gradually
effected, many of our cities now having Boards of Control.

The following extract from the Municipal Manual of the City of
Winnipeg states succinctly the organization of the city government
and the duties of the various officials and departments:

The government of the City is carried on under the powers of a
Charter from the Provincial Legislature. The Council is composed of
a Mayor, four Controllers, forming the Board of Control, and fourteen Aldermen. The Mayor and Controllers are elected annually
from a vote of the entire city. One Alderman is elected annually
from each of the seven wards into which the city is divided and
holds office for a term of two years. The Mayor is Chief Magistrate
of the City. Persons eligible for election as Mayor and Controller
must be owners of property, rated on the assessment roll of the City
to the value of two thousand dollars, over and above all encum-
brances against the same, and for Aldermen, must be rated in a like
manner, to the amount of five hundred dollars. The election is held
annually on the second Tuesday in December and nominations on
the first Tuesday in December.

The Council as a whole is the legislative body, and carried on its
legislative work through standing committees in the usual way.

The Board of Control is the executive body, and as such deals
with all financial matters, regulates and supervises expenditures,
revenues and investments, directs and controls departments, nomi-
nates all heads of departments, prepares specifications, advertises for
tenders for work, materials and supplies required, inspects and
reports to the Council upon all municipal works being carried on, or
in progress within the City, and generally administers the affairs of
the City, except as to the Public Schools and Police Department, the
former being under control of the Public School Board, elected
annually by the ratepayers, and the latter under the Board of Police

Commissioners, which consists of the Mayor, the County Court Judge, Police Magistrate and two Aldermen, appointed by the Council.

The Public Parks of the City are placed under the control and supervision of a Public Parks Board, composed of the Mayor, two members of the Council and six ratepayers appointed by the Council. For the purpose of providing for the expenditures required for Park purposes, a rate of one-half of one mill on the dollar may be levied on the general assessment of the City.

Many experiments looking to the perfecting of the machinery of city government are being tried elsewhere, notably in the United States, in recent years, and are being advocated in this country. Among these, one of the most important is the Commission Form of government, by which several commissioners elected by the people administer the affairs of the city. Each commissioner is head of a particular department. This arrangement, it is claimed, centralizes power, thus securing efficiency, and at the same time locates responsibility, so making public officials amenable to the will of the people. The carrying out of this plan involves the adoption of what is known as Direct Legislation. This includes (a) the Referendum, that is, the direct reference of proposed legislation to the people; (b) the Initiative, that is, the right of the people to initiate legislation; (c) the Recall, that is, the right of the people to dismiss an unsatisfactory official; (d) The Veto, that is, an effective protest by the people. Another group of proposed reforms frequently associated with these are, the Non-Partisan Primary, Election at large on a general ticket, Proportional Representation and Obligatory Voting.

Whatever the merits of these proposals — and they deserve serious consideration — it must be remembered that no mechanical device is a substitute for active and disinterested public opinion. Of greater importance than the perfection of the machine is the character of the people who operate it.

The securing of competent officials to carry on the business of the city is a difficult though most important matter. Ely (in *The Coming City*), draws attention to Continental methods. There a city will sometimes publicly advertise for a mayor, securing at a good salary, a man with special training and wide administrative experience.

All this seems strange to us, and it brings forcefully before us certain contrasts with our nineteenth-century notions of municipal government; but it points out to us, in at least a very general way, the direction in which our twentieth-century city is moving. The most marked contrasts with older thought may perhaps best be presented by these conclusions, which are suggested by our advertisement for a mayor:

1 Municipal government is a profession, not a business.
2 It is a difficult profession, requiring special preparation.
3 A man should devote his life to it.

The most noteworthy development of city life is the extension of the functions of government. In earlier times the cities exercised little more than police powers. As community ideals have developed there has gradually been forced upon the city the necessity for carrying on a great variety of communal enterprises. When the town pump was no longer adequate to the needs, it became evident that private enterprise could not provide a water supply efficiently or economically. So the city established a waterworks system. When it became impossible for each family to dispose of its own garbage, the city was forced to make provision for scavenging. So the volume of city business has been constantly growing.

Howe, in his *The City, the Hope of Democracy*, quotes from the Lord Mayor of Manchester:

The expansion of corporation activity is not likely to diminish in volume. The growth of municipal responsibilities illustrates the drift, and, as I believe, the irresistible drift of public affairs ... The democratic ideal is being worked out through municipalities. Communism and Socialism, words of terror a few short years ago, are finding a peaceful solution in various phases of municipal work. For what are free libraries, art galleries, baths, parks, technical schools, tramways, but communistic efforts? ... We need some stimulus to quicken our sense of the value of mutual helpfulness. The real resources, material and mental, of a city like ours are probably greater than were ever known in the world's history. Is it not possible to so direct these resources that the lives of all of us may be sweetened and made more tolerable? Some day men will awake to the immense possibilities of corporate action, and the community will find salvation, not in the patronage and gifts of the wealthy, but in the combined and intelligent efforts of the people themselves.

We must gain this new ideal of city government – an ideal that may best be expressed in a phrase of Prof. R. T. Ely, the city as a 'well ordered household.' As Jane Addams points out in her *Newer Ideals of Peace* the old military ideals of patriotism are being replaced by those of a rising concern for human welfare: 'A new history of government begins with an attempt to make life possible and human in large cities, in those crowded quarters which exhibit such an undoubted tendency to barbarism and degeneracy when the better human qualities are not nourished ... These paths lead to a type of government founded upon peace and fellowship as contrasted with restraint and defence.' Already we are entering upon the new era. The city is rapidly extending its activities and a new spirit is in the air. Glance over a modern city directory – Engineer of Construction, Power Construction Department, City Quarry, Parks Department, Playground Commission, Public Baths, Library Committee, Health Department, Hospital Committee, Building Inspector, and a score more. Or read a departmental report. I quote extracts from the 1909 Report of the Winnipeg Department of Public Health:

More effort has been put forward to control and eradicate tuberculosis during the past year than in any previous period during the city's history ... This department has been furnishing sputum cups and boxes free, when requested by the nurse or physician in attendance ... We have, as yet, touched only the fringes, but hope during the coming year to see many advances made, particularly along the line of education of the public by exhibitions, lectures and other means.

It is worthy of note that during the past year all the typhoid occurring in the city was what is sometimes called the residual type, that is, it was not due to infection carried by water or milk ... We are unable to recall any year in the past decade in which we did not have at least one well-marked outbreak, due to infection of a milk route ... We cannot but conclude that the increased vigilance which has been exercised over the milk supply, particularly with regard to illness at dairies, has had some effect ... The campaign against the fly has been prosecuted vigorously by doing away with its breeding-places as much as possible and by screening food exposed for sale, and by disinfecting houses where typhoid cases occur.

Pneumonia is said to flourish among an ill-fed, ill-clothed, badly-nourished population, especially when crowded together amid insanitary surroundings, with an insufficient supply of pure air and sunshine ... It is hoped that the new tenement house by-law, recently passed by your Council, may have an effect in lessening this high mortality. We would like, however, to have seen more adequate provisions made in this by-law to ensure ventilation of premises.

During the year regulations have been drafted and promulgated by the health committee, dealing with laundries. These were the means of effecting almost a revolution in the conditions which formerly obtained in the Chinese laundries of the city ... We are applying to the Legislature at the ensuing sessions for further powers relating to the prescribing of a standard for ice cream ...

Overcrowding notices totalled 1,852, an increase over last year, but most of these were not extreme cases, but merely verbal warnings of the Inspector, whose special duty this is; that the number of beds must be reduced, for it requires ceaseless vigilance to keep within bounds the temptation of certain classes to eke out a slender living by taking in boarders regardless of the size of their rooms or families.

Waste paper has become of a slight commercial value during the year, a revenue of $62.24 having been obtained from its sale ... This is a beginning, and we trust that the day is not far distant when other classes of so-called refuse collected by the scavengers will become marketable commodities and increase the city's revenue.

Smoke means waste, it also means that the atmosphere is fouled by unconsumed carbon (for black and gray smoke is really unconsumed carbon), which may militate against the public health in addition to its being a menace to the comfort of the individual ... Smoke nuisances have been abated at the following premises during the year ...

We try to impress upon restaurant proprietors that the best advertisement they can have is to throw their kitchens open to public inspection.

And so the Report proceeds, covering everything pertaining to the health of the citizens. Decidedly this is municipal housekeeping, and the head of such a department one of the best types of the social worker.

With this extension of civic work has come a greatly increased expenditure. How is this to be met? The answer to this question involves the many knotty problems of taxation, and behind that, theories of value.

Many thinkers believe that in what they term the 'unearned increment,' the city has an unlimited treasuretrove that is now being privately appropriated, but which rightly belongs to the community. Their position might be illustrated in some such way as this:

Suppose I have one hundred dollars to invest. On a holiday trip to the West I notice the rapid growth of the little towns, and decide to put my momey into a town-lot. So I return with the deed in my pocket. Five years later, I go to see my town-lot. The town has grown; people have come in from all parts; they have built houses and stores and churches and schools. My lot is now worth one thousand dollars. It was a good speculation. All it has cost me was a few dollars in taxes. Making allowance for the current rate of interest, I expended, at the outside figure, fifty dollars. If I sold, I could clear $850.00 on my investment. But why should I sell? I go away for another five years. At the end of that time the town has grown into a city. There are now waterworks and street cars and all the improvements of a modern city. My lot is now right in the business section and is, I am told, worth ten thousand dollars. I estimate my outlay at one thousand dollars. That enables me at one stroke to 'clean up' a neat nine thousand dollars. But to whom does that nine thousand dollars really belong? Of course, I have the deed of the land. But who created its value? Surely the whole community. In the meantime this community has piled up a vast indebtedness. This means heavy taxes for those who have built homes and are carrying on business. It means such a general high cost of living that newcomers can hardly obtain a foothold. I, having made no improvements, have escaped with a light tax. Being a non-resident I have not otherwise shared communal burdens. Surely there is something wrong here. Yes, I am in justice forced to admit that the taxes on my lot should have been heavier. How much heavier? Let us get back to values. The $9,000 which I 'made' *is community value and should have been retained by the community.* I have probably a right to my $1,000. I have no moral right whatever to the $9,000 – the 'unearned increment.' Have we here the key to a just system of

taxation? If not, wherein lies the fallacy in the foregoing argument?
Howe thus states the situation:

No act of the owner creates this value. Nothing which he can do will
increase or diminish it. It is proof against the elements; fire cannot
destroy it nor the winds or rain impair it. But every increase in
population, every dollar expended for improvements, sewers, streets,
lighting, police, fire or health protection adds its increment to the
value of building sites, or the privilege of occupying the city's highways. For the right of using the city's streets, for the supply of
transportation, gas, water, electric lighting and telephones is in all
respects like the site value of land. In the eyes of the law these are
appurtenances to the land. And the influences which enhance the
value of the land, increase the value of these franchises as well.

'It is this growing fund,' concludes Mr. Howe, 'this unearned
increment, which exists by virtue of the city and could not exist
without it, that offers a ready-made source of revenue for municipal
purposes.' It is of interest that Vancouver and several other Western
cities are experimenting with the so-called single tax, or a tax on the
land alone.

In the preceding quotations, reference is made to the city franchises and the rich revenue which they should yield to the city.
Perhaps the best way to secure this is not through taxation, but
through public services being operated directly by the city itself.

Here we enter upon the broader question of the granting of
special privileges and its corrupting effect on our city life.

Unfortunately on this continent the cities have allowed private
individuals and corporations to carry on and make immense profit
out of much of the business that legitimately belongs exclusively to
the city. Again quoting Howe:

In city and in state it is the greed for franchise grants and special
privileges that explains the worst of the conditions. This is the universal cause of municipal shame. By privilege, democracy has been
drugged. And this explanation is susceptible of deductive, as well as
inductive, proof. The franchises are the most valuable gift in the
possession of the city. Those to whom our cities have given millions,
those who have been enriched by the city's liberality, those who

have grown in wealth by the mere growth of population, have not
been content with the city's generosity; but like the serpent in the
fable, have turned and stung the breast of those who have befriended
them ... An examination of the conditions in city after city discloses
one sleepless influence that is common to them all. Underneath the
surface phenomena the activity of privilege appears, the privileges of
the street railway, the gas, the water, the telephone, and electric
lighting companies. The connection of these industries with politics
explains most of the corruption; it explains the power of the boss
and the machine; it suggests the explanation of the indifference of
the 'best' citizen and his hostility to democratic reform.

From our Canadian cities comes the same cry:

Montreal is a sufferer from the unsightly, often dangerous and
usually monopolistic utilization of modern public franchises —
electric tramways, lighting, telephones and telegraphs. Companies
organized to exploit these utilities have obtained the necessary
privileges from Legislature or Parliament, and often display scant
concern for the quality of their service to the city, notwithstanding
their use of its streets and highways. Hitherto, the companies, by
successful lobbying, have been able to prevent hostile or regulating
legislation. Hon. R. Stanley Weir, D.C.L., City Recorder, Montreal,
in *University of Toronto Studies*.

How has this condition arisen? Let me quote at length from
Wilcox's (*The American City*) admirable treatment of this subject:

The growth of cities and the progress of mechanical arts have
brought about improved methods of transportation, and given rise to
new and peculiar uses of the street. When the railway becomes as
absolutely essential in the common, everyday life of the people as
the wagon road is — and that day seems to be at hand for city people
at any rate — it may come to be considered as anomalous to have
privately owned railways as it is now to have private roads ...
Monopolies and special privileges controlled by private persons for
selfish ends, where they involve the power to tax the common necessities of life, are, of course, inimical to democracy, both in theory
and in practice ... Private ownership of the facilities for transporta-

tion can be tolerated under such circumstances only when ownership
is so far subordinated to public control as to be, in fact, conditional.
Strictly speaking, under the conditions of life in a great city, private
ownership is impossible. These facilities are so public in their very
nature, that law itself cannot successfully contravene this fact and
make them private ... The streets of a city are such an essential asset
of its free citizens that it is questionable whether a municipal corporation should ever grant the right to any private parties to place
fixtures in the highways. At least, any such rights, if granted, should
be strictly limited in their term and the manner of their exercise, and
should be revocable whenever public interest demands. A condition
of affairs where a private company can fight the city on a claim of
rights in the streets, in perpetuity, or for a term of years, on the
strength of some doubtful or implied grant, is well nigh intolerable.
Furthermore, practically all these services which require special
privileges in the streets are of such general importance as to demand
that their performance be very nearly at cost. Cheap water, light and
transportation have come to be almost as essential a condition of life
in cities as free highways.

When cities are young, and public utilities, the need of which is
sorely felt, are still in the experimental stage commercially, citizens
are inclined to favor making any concessions and granting any privileges that will bring about the desired improvements and bring them
quickly. Under such conditions the first franchises in most American
cities were given away. After a time private promoters began to see
that a franchise had monetary value, especially if it was for a long
term of years in a growing city, and subject to conditions that would
make the utility self-supporting at the start. When common councils
got hold of this idea, the era opened in which promoters found it
more convenient to pay a part of the value of a franchise to the
aldermen as individuals, than to pay the whole of it into the city
treasury. After the people at large woke up to the fact that franchises granted on desirable conditions are valuable, a third era began
to dawn, the era of agitation for the sale of franchises, so that the
people as a whole should get some return for the right which they
grant.

Most of our Canadian cities are still at the earlier stages of this
process. But why should we continue to allow the profits that are

Polish and Russian immigrant types

essentially public to go into private pockets? 'Our cities,' says Rauschenbusch, 'have surrendered nearly all the functions that bring an income, keeping only those that demand expenditure.'

Where lies the blame? In part, perhaps an antiquated theory of government, a rapid and unforeseen development of urban life, the incoming of an ignorant and untrained population, and the clever manipulations of unscrupulous promoters; but more largely the selfish indifference of the majority of the citizens.

In *The Shame of the Cities,* an *exposé* of 'graft' in American city life, Lincoln Steffens concludes, 'The misgovernment of the American people is misgovernment by the American people ... The business man has failed in politics as he has in citizenship. Why? Because politics is business. That's what's the matter with it. The commercial spirit is the spirit of profit, not patriotism; of credit, not honor; of individual gain, not national prosperity; of trade and dickering, not principle.'

Wickett refers to 'the tardy growth of Canada's population,' and 'the homogeneity of Canada's population' as two of the factors that have made for good government in our Canadian cities. He states that in Toronto, in 1902, ninety-eight and one-half per cent. were British born; only one-half of one per cent. came from the United States, and but one per cent. from other non-British countries.

Within a decade the situation is absolutely changed, even in Toronto. Our cities are growing by leaps and bounds and the newcomers belong to many nationalities.

As far back as the year 1907 — and that is a long time at the rate things have been moving — Hon. P. G. Martineau, Judge of the Superior Court for the Province of Quebec, wrote of Montreal:

Montreal with 34,966 inhabitants of English origin, 37,077 Irish, 18,108 Scotch, 163,034 French, 2,911 Germans, 1,633 Italians, 4,932 Jews; with 202,091 Catholics and 53,595 Protestants; with the French living principally in one part of the city, the English in another, and the Irish in another; with enough of each nationality in each ward to keep the balance of power and to materially affect the result of election; with most of the industrial capital belonging to the minority, the laboring forces to the majority, Montreal occupies certainly a unique position. The following words of Prof. Edward J. James in an address before the National Conference for good city government in Minneapolis in 1894, are here particularly apt: 'The mixture of many nationalities, the lack of homogeneousness in the population, has made the problem of city government infinitely more difficult than it otherwise would have been. You may take good elements from half a dozen good populations, throw them together into one political community, and immediately a new set of difficulties in the government of that community will arise, because of lack of homogeneity of political ideals and of intellectual sympathies.' These conditions exist in Montreal, and explain many otherwise incomprehensible phases of its annals. Traces of nationalism are found everywhere – in the charter, in committees, in the distribution of patronage, in general administration, in the press, coming unexpectedly to the surface and again disappearing under the influence of toleration and tact. 'Civic Administration of Montreal,' *University of Toronto Studies,* vol. II., no 4.

Conditions similar to those that are developing with us produced in the United States the city 'Boss,' the 'Spoils System,' and the party 'Machine.' What about our Canadian cities? Already we have had revelations of municipal corruption, of the party machine in our civic elections, of the 'handling' of the foreign vote and of the demoralizing influence of powerful interests. Unless we as Canadian citizens awake to the sense of our responsibilities and are willing to sacrifice our personal interests for the public welfare, we cannot hope to escape the disastrous experiences through which other cities have passed. We still have a fighting chance.

REFERENCES

'The City, the Hope of Democracy'
Frederic C. Howe. New York: Charles Scribner's Sons
'The American City'
Delos F. Wilcox. New York: The Macmillan Co.
'City Government in the United States'
Frank J. Goodnow. New York: Young People's Missionary Movement
'The Coming City'
Richard T. Ely. New York: Thomas Y. Crowell & Co.

'The Hindrances to Good Citizenship'
James Bryce. New Haven: Yale University Press
'Newer Ideals of Peace'
Jane Addams. New York: The Macmillan Co.
'The Shame of the Cities'
Lincoln Steffens. New York: Young People's Missionary Movement
'Progressive Taxation in Theory and Practice'
E. R. A. Seligman. New York: The Macmillan Co.
'Natural Taxation'
T. G. Shearman. New York: Doubleday, Page & Co.
University of Toronto Studies. Vol. 2
Reports of City Departments

Chapter 8

The seamy side or social pathology

And when Jesus drew nigh, he saw the city and wept over it.

Luke

A PARABLE

Said Christ our Lord, 'I will go and see
How the men, My brethren, believe in Me.'
He passed not again through the gate of birth,
But made Himself known to the children of earth.

Then said the chief priests, and rulers and kings,
'Behold, now, the Giver of all good things;
Go to, let us welcome with pomp and state
Him who alone is mighty and great!'

With carpets of gold the ground they spread
Wherever the Son of man should tread,
And in palace chambers lofty and rare
They lodged Him, and served Him with kingly fare.

Great organs surged through arches dim
Their jubilant floods in praise of Him,
And in church and palace and judgment hall
He saw His image high over all.

But still wherever His steps they led
The Lord in sorrow bent down His head,
And from under the heavy foundation stones
The Son of Mary heard bitter groans.

And in church and palace and judgment hall
He marked great fissures that rent the wall
And opened wider and yet more wide
As the living foundation heaved and sighed.

'Have ye founded your thrones and altars, then,
On the bodies and souls of living men?
And think ye that building shall endure
Which shelters the noble and crushes the poor?

'With gates of silver and bars of gold
Ye have fenced My sheep from their Father's fold;
I have heard the dropping of their tears
In heaven, these eighteen hundred years.

'O Lord and Master, not ours the guilt,
We built but as our fathers built;
Behold Thine images, how they stand,
Sovereign and sole, through all our land.

'Our task is hard — with sword and flame
To hold Thy earth forever the same,
And with sharp crooks of steel to keep
Still, as Thou leftest them, Thy sheep.'

Then Christ sought out an artisan,
A low-browed, stunted, haggard man,
And a motherless girl, whose fingers thin
Pushed from her faintly want and sin.

These set He in the midst of them,
And as they drew back their garment hem
For fear of defilement, 'Lo here,' said He,
'The images ye have made of me!'

Lowell

The following clippings tell their own story and make their own appeal. Women who have true sympathy and men who are not devoid of all chivalry cannot but feel impelled to do something to relieve the misery and banish the evils which are so prevalent in our midst. This chapter may be likened to a walk through a hospital. A detailed study of the various diseases, their cause and development, their treatment and the best means of prevention, is manifestly impossible here. But perhaps this hospital visit may incite us to clean up our back yards! In mixed study classes it may be advisable for the men and the women to conduct separate conferences on some aspects of the problems touched.

Crime Increases in Urban Centres — Ottawa, Ont., November 6th —
There was during the fiscal year 1908-9 a decided increase in the number of convicts from urban centres, due, no doubt, to the financial depression and lack of employment, but for the country districts the statistics as to criminality do not show much change ... In the report the assertion is made that the parole system is the most important and useful reform yet introduced. *Press Despatch.*

Winnipeg police statistics, 1910

OFFENCE

Assault	14	Breach of electric by-law	8
Assault and battery	322	Breach of Lord's Day	
Assault occ. bodily harm	41	by-law	83
Attempted theft	—	Breach of various	
Attempted murder	9	by-laws	234
Attempted fraud	1	Carry revolver	30
Assaulting peace officer	18	Cruelty to animals	44
Abusive language	1	Carnal knowledge girl	
Attempted rape	1	under 14	18
Attempted burglary	3	Contribute to delin. of	
Aid and abet in theft	1	juvenile	1
Aggravated assault	1	Challenge to prize fight	1
Attempted personation	1	Cause explosion to	
Attempted carnal		endanger life	1
knowledge	1	Cause bodily harm by	
Aid and abet dog fight	1	neglect of duty	4
Attempted robbery	2	Drunk on street	3,033
Attempt to procure case		Drunk and disorderly	397
seduction	2	Disorderly	423
Attempted gross indecency	1	Discharge firearms	10
Attempted to engage in		Driving motor while drunk	1
prize fight	2	Circulating obscene matter	3
Attempted shop-breaking	1	Defamatory libel	2
Burglary	1	Driving at immoderate rate	7
Bigamy	1	Deserting employment	2
Breach of health by-law	595	Drunk on railway duty	2
Breach of street by-law	1,461	Demanding money with	
Breach of early closing		intent to steal	6
by-law	160	Exhibiting immoral	
Breach of license by-law	160	play	2
Breach of parks by-law	61	Executing valuable	
Breach pound by-law	36	security by fraud	1
Breach dairy by-law	35	Escape from lawful	
Breach of bakery by-law	4	custody	8
Breach of plumbing by-law	2	Forgery and uttering	28
Breach of militia by-law	2	Forgery and attempting	
Breach building by-law	75	to utter	8

Forgery	3	Operating street car	
Fraud	46	while drunk	1
Frequenting bawdy house	1	Obstructing peace officer	8
Harboring vicious dog	4	Obstructing sanitary	
Housebreaking with		constable	1
intent	1	Obstructing street	
Housebreaking with		railway constable	1
theft	10	Playing or looking on in	
Indecent assault	9	gaming house	172
Inmate of bawdy house	56	Pointing revolver	7
Inmate of disorderly house	3	Procuring	5
Indecent act	—	Perjury	2
Interdiction	1	Refuse to pay wages	216
Incest	1	Refuse to pay livery	13
Inmate of opium joint	15	Rape	4
Interfering with railway		Receiving stolen goods	9
signals	1	Riding on railway	
In possession of stolen		watchman's ticket	11
goods	1	Refusing to pay chimney	
Keeping bawdy house	56	sweep	5
Keeping gaming house	13	Robbery	13
Keeping opium joint	4	Seduction	7
Keeping resort for		Shopbreaking and theft	11
prostitutes	3	Selling of cigarettes to	
Murder	3	minors	1
Material witnesses	4	Supplying drugs for	
Manslaughter	2	unlawful purposes	1
Neglect to support children	1	Theft	422
Neglect to support wife	2	Theft of post letters	2
Neglect of duty endanger-		Theft from dwelling-	
ing life	2	house	4
Owning vicious dog	9	Theft from person	13
Obtaining money by false		Trespass	9
pretences	36	Throwing missile at	
Obtaining credit by false		street car	8
pretences	7	Using threatening	
Obtaining goods by false		language	41
pretences	4	Using insulting language	19
Obtaining board by false		Unlawfully selling cocaine	3
pretences	1	Unlawfully wounding	3

Using profanity on		Witnesses	9
street	1	Wounding with intent	8
Vagrancy	640	Summary arrests	406
Wilful damage	53	Arrests on warrant	158

Telegram, Jan. 10th, 1911

Nationalities represented in above

American	384	Halfbreed	261
Austrian	16	Hungarian	11
Assyrian	3	Irish	540
Africander	2	Italian	37
Australian	2	Icelander	39
Bukowinian	13	Indian	5
Belgian	9	Jew	21
Bohemian	8	Norwegian	74
Canadian	1,343	New Zealander	6
Chinamen	122	Newfoundlander	2
Dutch	28	Polish	248
English	1,092	Ruthenian	347
French-Canadian	151	Russian	51
French	35	Roumanian	16
Finlander	8	Scotch	845
German	113	Swede	118
Galician	43	Swiss	1
Greek	4	Welsh	26

Total			6,024

(Police Report)

Slums result from three causes, lack of regulation and supervision on the part of the city, the greed of land-owners, and the necessities of the poor.

Webster's Dictionary says that the word 'slum' is supposed to be a contraction of the word 'asylum,' and is a back street of a city, especially one filled with a poor, dirty and vicious population.

This is only a partial definition, for a street, so long as it is a street, can with a little effort be redeemed from the slum condition. No, the slum is something worse than a back street; it is a lane or

City back-yards

The yard room to these houses is only a few square feet
Unsanitary slaughter house
The first house has three flats; stairs on the outside give entrance to each

alley, a series of lots about one hundred and fifty feet deep, with
three or four houses, hovels or shacks erected, one behind the other,
and entirely hidden from the view of the ordinary passerby. It is a
place where stables, barns and sheds have been converted into residences, not for one, but often for two or three families, with none
of the ordinary requirements of home life.

In earlier days, men were either passively allowed, or took permission, to erect rows of lath and plaster cottages on lanes not fifteen
feet wide; yards were divided and subdivided until in some districts
there is a perfect labyrinth of hovels, absolutely lacking in sanitary
conveniences, and in various stages of dilapidation and decay. Such
a thing as 'repairs' is never dreamed of, for the rent can be obtained
all the same, and to fix up looks like unnecessary extravagance.
The household refuse, slops, dishwater, etc., are thrown outside the
door to sow the diseases that daily attack the inmates, sending
adults to the hospital and babies to the graveyard.

One could find in his heart some measure of sympathy and
acquiescence if the hovels were built and owned by the poor themselves, but these places are owned by well-to-do citizens who sin
against their city from avaricious motives, and live in luxury on the
exorbitant rents imposed on the poor and comfortless occupants.
J. J. Kelso, in *Can Slums be Abolished?*

It is true not only of the world, but of this city, that one-half does
not know how the other half lives; to thousands in Toronto a knowledge of conditions in the 'Ward,' so far as housing conditions are
concerned, would come as a surprise and shock. The words of Rev.
Benjamin Gregory, of Manchester, that 'there is nothing in that city
to compare with the housing conditions in Toronto,' and the words
of another, that 'London itself does not present such conditions,'
should arouse the interest of worthy citizens and lead to serious
inquiry. It is safe to say the worst conditions cannot be readily seen
by the slum visitor, but even a general view of conditions must convince anyone of the criminal carelessness of any community which
permits such conditions to exist, much more to continue.

Here is one instance: A dirty hovel, the floor of which is broken
down toward the middle, so that it rests on the ground, and on the
floor water stagnates for many months of the year. In it are three
apartments bearing the semblance of rooms, and in these a family

consisting of father, mother, four children, and a boarder manage to exist. The father has been out of work for months; the mother, soon to bear again the responsibility of motherhood, goes out daily to earn a partial support for the family by doing janitor work. In another case, in surroundings almost similar, we find the father has been ill for months, and the mother looks so — the wonder is that it could be otherwise. The eldest son, a mere child, is a criminal, returning regularly to the hands of the police, and this is what we might expect. In neither house referred to are there any sanitary conveniences. These two typical places to which we have referred can be called neither homes nor houses.

Then, let anyone take a general view of the surroundings and be convinced that here is the festering sore of our city life. The lanes, alleyways and back yards are strewn with refuse, houses behind houses, and in the yards between unsightly piles of ramshackle out-houses that are supposed to provide sanitary conveniences — some of these reeking with filth and stench. Then let some one not already convinced walk through these surroundings when the rain has fallen and the hot sun beats down, and smell the smoke of their torment that ascends continually, and we would hear such a protest as would cause some action to be taken. We are told that in the midst of all this these poor people pay ten or twelve dollars per month for these miserable rambling hovels that would not sell for fifty dollars apiece. Rev. H. S. Magee, in *Christian Guardian*.

We are told that we have no slum district in Toronto and know nothing about the tenement house; but we do know that there is a great deal of overcrowding, and the effect on the children is something that we will realize better later on. I fear that Toronto is breeding a class of criminals that will keep it busy to take care of in the next few years, if nothing is done. The effect on children as regards their health is very bad. Our work is all among the poor, and only yesterday one of our workers went to a home where father, mother and five children were living in two rooms. One child was tubercular. They were sleeping four in one bed, and the sick child on a couch. These children sleep in the living-room. There was another case where a child was born in one of these homes. The mother was in an advanced stage of tuberculosis, and father, mother and four children slept in a room 10 ft. x 12 ft. The kitchen was a mite of a place only large enough for a stove, table and chairs. These people living in this huddled condition and with no precaution whatever taken against this disease, you can imagine what chance these children have ...

Close to our mission there is a family of seven — three of these are grown-up girls — living in a tiny cottage, and they have a man border living with them. I don't know what chance there is for these girls, and next door to them is a family consisting of father, mother and two growing children. They have seventeen men boarders and only one accommodation.

I know of another case where a girl and boy were adopted — not brother and sister — and as there were a number of other children in this house, they occupied the same room until the boy was 19 and the girl 16 or 17, and to-day she is one of the most difficult problems we have in our mission. She is bold and brazen, no soft spot in her. But what else could you expect! She was reared where a blessing was asked at table, but I ask you what chance had she to grow up virtuously in a crowded place like that. I leave it to your own imagination how horrible the conditions are where the father or mother drink, or perhaps both, huddled in these close quarters? Is it not natural that we should find many children practising vice? Our hearts ache for them but we are helpless. We have one family not far from our mission where the woman drinks and is thoroughly immoral. She has a little boy about ten years of age threatened with tuberculosis. He was in the hospital and they said his only chance was good nourishment, the best of care and lots of fresh air, but in this place there is no possible ventilation. They live in two little rooms, and there are two or three women of disreputable character who have two other little boys. We come across so much of that kind of thing in our work, and yet people cannot believe that such a state of affairs exists in Toronto. Miss Charity Cook, *Conference Charities and Correction*, 1909.

Five-cent boarders don't bring in an awful lot of money, but when there is a crowd of them some return is shown. This fact explains why two overcrowding cases came up in the court this morning.

Mrs. M. Chudek found that her rates were low, but when she secured a big bunch for her house at a time she found it was a paying proposition. Still she has to put an item of $20.00 and costs to her profit and loss account when she balances her books, for this was her fine in court this morning.

The health inspector rudely paid a midnight visit to the place at 47 Austin street the other night, the place being where Mrs. Chudek runs her boarding-house.

There he found thirty-two men living, where there should be seven, according to the laws of health. Scientists say that in a room where human beings live, there should be 400 cubic feet of air space to each man. In Mrs. Chudek's house it worked out at 91 cubic feet to each occupant, a fact which, not only being uncomfortable, was dangerous to the human health.

There were four rooms and each filled literally to the roof. The boarders were located in rooms as follows:

One room, 13 ft. by 8 ft. by 8 ft., 6 occupants; should be 2.
One room, 12 ft. by 8 ft. by 8 ft., 6 occupants; should be 2.
One room, 13 ft. by 9 ft. by 8 ft., 8 occupants; should be 2.
One room, 13 ft. by 12 ft. by 7 ft., 12 occupants; should be 2½.

Figured out, this means there are thirty-two people where there should be seven, and each gets 91 cubic feet of air, instead of 400.

If these people had even kept the place decent at all, the case might not be quite so bad, but in the words of the health officer, it was 'filthy.' The bedclothes, chairs and everything in the rooms were covered with dirt.

In handling this case, the magistrate addressed the woman and said: 'People are supposed to live like human beings and not like hogs. In your house there was not space for a dog, let alone a man. Besides being overcrowded the place was abominably filthy and as a starter I'll fine you twenty dollars and costs.'

Another case just as bad was that of M. and P. Kozuchar, who conduct a boarding-house at 37 Austin street and who were following the example of the other defendant in packing their house like a box of sardines. In this case the rooms were allotted as follows:

1 room, 11 x 14 x 7, four men and two girls; should be two.
1 room, 18½ x 15 x 7, twelve men; should be five.
1 room, (in cellar) 15 x 14 x 6, seven men; should not be occupied.

The worst of this case was that men and girls were sleeping in the same room and that the cellar was occupied as a living-room. In all there were twenty-five people where there should be only seven. The

magistrate scored the defendant severely and said he was going to
stop this sort of thing. He administered a fine of ten dollars and
costs. Winnipeg *Telegram*, Oct. 15th, 1909.

The cells at police headquarters were filled to their utmost capacity
last night, no less than seventy men, besides a number of women,
finishing up their Thanksgiving celebrations behind the bars. A
number of others were bailed by their friends, and judging from the
number of battered and bleeding faces seen in the station duty
office, there were others who ought to have been there and some of
whom likely will be.

A reporter who visited the cells at 3 o'clock this morning found
that less than half of the prisoners were provided with beds. There
are seventeen cells for male prisoners, and these were so crowded
that many of the men were spending the night lying on the concrete
floor, while others paced to and fro behind the bars like wild beasts
in a cage. Some prisoners lay in a drunken sleep; others, half-
sobered, made night hideous with their attempts to sing, 'We shall
meet on that beautiful shore' being the favorite hymn at the time
the reporter called. Among the prisoners were a few sober, respect-
ably dressed men, and with no bed, no quiet and the company of
drunken cell-mates, they appeared to have little cause for thanksgiving. *Winnipeg Free Press*, Oct. 25th, 1909.

A knife, a girl and a Galician boarding-house this morning made a
foundation for an interesting story in the police court. John Sorocki
was charged with unlawfully wounding Michael Katsuk during a
fight which they had in their boarding-house, 4 Austin street, May
23. The wounded man was in the General Hospital for five days and
then went out, and had to pay visits to have his wounds dressed. The
trouble arose over a pretty Galician girl. And while they did not
fight there and then about her, ill-feeling had been caused between
the two men. They fought on the streets May 23, and the lady saw
them at it, but it did not seem to worry her in the least. In the afternoon of the same day they came together again and this time the
fight was a good deal more serious.

After a few desultory passes Katsuk ran away. He saw a small
knife glittering in the hand of his one-time friend. This was taken
from the infuriated Sorocki, but seeing a large carving-knife on the

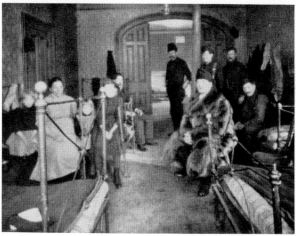

Interiors of some 'homes'

Bedroom, kitchen, yard, everything in one
An example of overcrowding

table he grabbed it and made three or four vicious cuts at Katsuk as
he was getting through the door. The wounds were very painful and
one of them was three inches long and half an inch deep. The
wounded man was removed to the General Hospital, where he remained for five days. None of the wounds proved dangerous unless
neglected. In court this morning, seven witnesses gave evidence of
the fights in the morning and evening, and told how Sorocki had
slashed at Katsuk as he was escaping through the door of the
kitchen. Sorocki was sentenced to nine months' imprisonment.
Winnipeg *Telegram*, June 23.

In a dingy little three-roomed house on Stella Avenue, with a
smoking 32-calibre Colt's automatic revolver dropping from his
nerveless grasp as he sank to the floor in his last sleep, Henry
Schwartz, a Polish Galician, who has lived many years in Winnipeg,
and has been accounted in his day a successful business man and a
good citizen, put a tragic and bloody finale to his chequered life
history this morning shortly before 9 o'clock. Within a few feet of
him lay the lifeless body of the woman who for four years passed as
his wife in this country, the mother of his three children, who are
now in the Children's Home, all unconscious of the fate that has
overtaken their parents. Away in Galicia, the far country from which
Schwartz returned only last night, there is, in the municipality of
Sambor, a neglected grave that contains the mortal remains of four
other human beings who owed their sudden and unnatural deaths to
the same Henry Schwartz. After pumping bullets into the body of his
Winnipeg wife, killing her instantly, Schwartz turned the revolver on
himself, and completed his apparently premeditated plan of murder
and suicide this morning.

   According to the information given by friends and neighbors,
Schwartz left Winnipeg about four months ago for Galicia, deserting his
supposed wife and their three young children. Prior to his leaving, the
life of the couple had been anything but happy, as the Winnipeg wife
had heard tales of another wife and family in the old country, and
kept urging and insisting that Schwartz do something to give her her
legal and rightful position. At that time they lived at 107½ Grove
Street, where Schwartz kept a busy little grocery store. The deserted
woman struggled to make a living for her three children, but some
three weeks ago the Children's Aid stepped in and took her little

brood away from her. She had moved to the house, 479 Stella
Avenue, where she met her tragic death this morning. Meantime
Schwartz had got back to his old home at Sambor, in Galicia, and
had found that the wife and four children that he deserted there
were all dead. Old friends told him the sordid story of how the
deserted woman fought to keep life in her pitiable home, only to
give up the struggle and end it all with poison, which she gave to all
four of the children before killing herself. *Winnipeg Free Press,* Feb.
9th, 1910.

Table showing nationality of children cared for by the Children's
Aid Society of Winnipeg during the past eight years, including
present year:

American	25	Hungarian	4
Austrian	5	Irish	46
Australian	2	Negro	1
Canadian	322	Polish	59
Dutch	2	Russian	14
English	150	Ruthenian	4
French	7	Roumanian	1
French half-breeds	30	Swedish	8
Galician	58	Scotch	34
German	43	Welsh	6
Icelandic	6	Unknown	1
Total			828

The following summaries of cases dealt with are taken at random
as typical of the work the Society is doing:

1071 was a little girl seven years of age, whose mother and father
were dead. Three years previous to her death, the mother had been
living a very immoral life, and consequently this little child had been
sadly neglected. When taken over by the Society, she was in a very
deplorable condition, but within a very short time she was transformed into a different girl. She turned out to be a very obedient,
willing little girl, and a suitable foster-home was soon found for her,
where she is now doing remarkably well.

1078 was a little Polish girl said to be eleven years of age, who had been deserted by her father. This little child states her mother died in the country some time ago, and that her new mother was very unkind to her. It was found out later that this woman was living in adultery with the child's father. The father brought her to Winnipeg, leaving her in charge of some Polish people; since then he has never been heard of. The little child was handed from this family to another, who treated her in a very brutal manner. She finally endeavored to better her own condition, and went off in search of employment, and landed at one of the City's employment bureaus, who notified the Society about her. This little child was in a filthy condition, her hair being completely matted together. She was, however, soon given an opportunity of removing her filth and rags, and after spending hours on her hair it was transformed from one matted mass to a luxuriant head of hair, of which I may say she is very proud now. This little one became a most loving and affectionate child, and all connected with her transformation were very sorry indeed when the day came for her to go to a foster-home. Excellent reports are received from her.

1009-10-11-12-13-14. Neglected and destitute was the condition of a family, consisting of six small children, four boys and two girls, ranging in age from 2 to 12 years, and living in a country place thirty miles out of Winnipeg, which was brought to the Society's notice. The Society, on hearing of this case, immediately dispatched one of its officers with a supply of clothing, etc. After having procured sufficient evidence to warrant his action, this officer had the case brought before the local magistrate, and the Society became the legal guardians of this family. On investigation the following facts were revealed: It appears the mother died about fifteen months ago, and the father, being of a very shiftless character and having no thought or love for his children, decided that he would make good his escape, and leave these poor little innocent ones to the mercy of the world. On hearing of the father's desertion, the neighbors took pity on the helpless little children, sheltered and fed them temporarily, thinking the father would ultimately return. This expectation was not realized, and the children became wards of the Society. Good homes have been found for them, and excellent reports of their progress have been received.

1047. This little girl, twelve years of age, was found in a boarding-house in the city, where she had been left by her father, who,

Two families of children – now in the care of the Children's Aid Society

informing the landlady that he was going to get a cheque cashed to
enable him to pay for her maintenance, went out, and has never
been seen since. After failing in every effort to find the father, the
Society placed the child in a good foster-home, where she is loved
and cared for. *Annual Report,* 1909-10.

In connection with the arrest yesterday of ____, alias ____, of the
underworld, charged with keeping a disorderly house, at 264 Main
Street, a state of affairs was revealed that fortunately has never
before been known in Winnipeg. Although the facts did not come
out when the woman pleaded guilty and was fined $50 and costs
with the option of three months in jail, it is stated that her place has
been a regular 'hang out' for messenger boys of all ages from 15 to
18 or 20, and that some of the boys were accustomed to spending
nearly all their spare time at the place. The woman, it is stated, paid
the boys trifling sums for running messages, washing dishes,
sweeping floors and other work about the place, but allowed them
to frequent her rooms any time they came around. Some of the boys
who are on night duty have admitted that they spent most of their
mornings and afternoons in the house 'just for the fun of the thing.'
The woman is a confirmed drug fiend. ____, arrested in connection
with the same place, appeared in court in a terrible condition from
the effects of morphine and a recent attack of pneumonia. Her case
was adjourned. *Winnipeg Free Press,* Feb. 4th, 1910.

There were 700 women last year in Toronto who assumed the duties
of motherhood without being able to enter into its joys. Miss
Sutliffe, of Ottawa, at Y.W.C.A. Conference, Elgin House, 1910.

During the last three years, 302 maternity cases have been sheltered
... (in the Haven, Toronto).

    Of these 302 cases, 102 were married women, in need of help and
shelter only through desertion or poverty, so they may be counted
out of our study.

    From the 200 cases of illegitimate motherhood were born fully
90 defective and diseased children. Of these, 35 have to my knowledge died in different institutions of this city — some with us, some
in the various hospitals, and others in the Infants' Home. Several
growing too old for our nursery are now in other institutions, and

several have been lost sight of through being taken in charge by relatives.

Of the 200 mothers, 132, or nearly three-fourths, were feeble-minded, and 137, or about the same proportion, were absolutely alone and friendless. A few, it is true, were hopelessly immoral, and a few were not bad, led away by their affections. Nearly all were either friendless or feeble-minded, therefore it is the general make-up of these two classes which we will study for a few moments. And in studying them, let us remember one thing, we are all of pretty much the *same human nature*. These poor souls are where we would be in the same circumstances and under the same influences – 'the colonel's lady and Biddy O'Grady are sisters under their skins!' I often say in my heart: 'But for the grace of God – which includes good heredity and environment – but for the grace of God there goes _____.' On the other hand I have seen gleams of the Divine life in a poor soul whose life had been, beyond expression, immoral! Even the worst of them, when you think for one moment of the generations of vice behind them, are only to be pitied and protected.

To begin with, girls of normal intelligence, but homeless, unrestrained – in the case of immigrants, unaccustomed to the freedom of a new country – it goes like wine to their heads, and they lose all sense of propriety or safety. Therefore, we frequently have girls who in the old countries have lived virtuous and respected lives – often bringing over with them the best of references – coming out here and *falling*, during the first few months. All alone and unprotected, and with no idea of the dangers in the way, they become an easy prey – generally to some one from 'home.' One good and true-hearted English girl came out here to be married to her lover, to whom she had been engaged for some time. She had with her her wedding clothes and her wedding presents! She went to live for a few days in a boarding-house, until arrangements could be completed for their wedding. She had no friends, and only her bedroom in which to receive her lover's visits. He being a scoundrel and she being weak, the usual thing happened. He deserted her forthwith – and there she is now, thousands of miles from home and family – with her poor little diseased baby in her arms! Her whole life ruined ...

In the good days to come, when we have Vigilance Committees looking after the morals of every lonely camp, and Morality

Societies, such as have been organized in some few of our towns, to
unearth the hidden strongholds of vice and to protect the weak and
lift up the fallen, and bring them back to God again; when our
Government at last recognizes and lifts the burden of its duty in
protecting the feeble-minded as well as the insane; and especially in
that Golden Age ahead, when no double standards of morality will
be tolerated, we shall look back upon the early days of the poor,
benighted twentieth century as to the darkness of the Middle Ages.
But it will be remembered that even then Love Divine stirred in the
hearts of men and women, causing them to make a noble fight
against these evils, and for the purification and right development of
the sources of humanity. So let us work and hope and trust, and 'put
a cheerful courage on,' never for one moment forgetting that in the
hearts of the defective, and even of the depraved, there is yet a
chord that responds to the Divine touch:
  'In the mud and scum of things,
    There always, always something sings.'
                                    Lucy W. Brooking, Supt. The Haven

John Bratton was indicted before Judge Myers yesterday afternoon
with unlawfully procuring a woman named Maud ＿＿＿ to become a
common prostitute. A conviction followed, and the judge, taking
into consideration that accused had already been in jail for five
months and on the understanding that he would be deported,
sentenced him to one month's imprisonment.
    Maud ＿＿＿ , who is seventeen years of age, went into the box and
told the court how she had met Bratton at Grand Forks, North
Dakota, early in July of last year, together with her cousin Edna.
Bratton was to marry her cousin and they were all to come to
Winnipeg for that purpose, and she, the witness, was to act as bridesmaid. They arrived in Winnipeg on July 7th, and went to live with a
Mrs. Stone at an address she could not remember. After they had
been there a week, Bratton suggested that they should go to another
boarding-house, which proved to be an address on McFarlane Street,
where the keeper told her she was too young to be admitted. They
then applied at 167 Rachel Street, kept by Alma Stanton, but here
also they would not admit her on account of her age. Eventually
she stayed at the house of a colored woman on McFarlane Street,
and all the money she received she handed over to the accused. She

remained there two days, and then accompanied the accused to
Brandon, Moose Jaw, Medicine Hat, Taber and several other places
where the same thing occurred, eventually returning to Winnipeg,
where Bratton was arrested.

Alma Stanton testified to accused coming to her house on Rachel
Street. He wanted to make arrangements with her, she said, to admit
Maud _____. Accused by his conversation knew very well what sort
of house she was keeping. She did not agree to his suggestion, as
Maud _____ was too young. *Winnipeg Free Press.*

A revolting story of procuring for immoral purposes was unfolded in
the police court this morning. It developed in the evidence against
Louis Liew, alias Maroff, who is charged with procuring Ethel _____.
He even went to the extent of marrying his victim. Directly after the
marriage he engaged and furnished a room in the Conway block on
Main Street, and within one week after his marriage, by threats and
beatings, forced his young wife of only seventeen years of age, to
live the life of the underworld.

Ethel _____, a pretty young Jewess, when called into the box this
morning, was almost prostrated with terror of the man who sat
facing her in the dock. Every few moments, after looking around in
an affrighted manner, she would lick her parched lips and would
turn with pleading eyes to the magistrate, as her small hands played
nervously along the edges of the witness box. In spite of all efforts,
nothing could be drawn from her at first, so completely was she
dominated by the man in the dock. The prisoner is not over twenty-
three, short and stout. Finally she whispered to the interpreter that
she would tell the court about it, and the magistrate stepped down
from his place on the bench to the edge of the box ...

Liew, or Maroff, is an example of the notorious New York
'Cadet' of whom so much has been written of late, and who makes a
substantial livelihood by procuring young and innocent women for
immoral purposes.

Ethel first met the accused at a theatre in the north end. In a very
short time, he, by the usual methods of pretending to have lots of
money and making her presents of cheap rings, which to her
untutored mind were exquisite gems, induced her to leave her home
which she was making some six weeks ago with her brother-in-law
at _____ . She had always been a good girl, a steady worker and

economical. Even now her brother holds $40 for her which she was saving to send for her mother in the Old Country, which Ethel had left three years ago.

Suddenly, without warning, she was missed one night from supper, and when she did come back late, she was wearing cheap rings, and as she stepped through the door of her home she told her panic-stricken sister that she was now a bride. She took her little bundle of clothes that night and went to live with her husband in the Conway Block. In a few hours under pressure and beatings from the husband she commenced the life that she continually told him she wanted to stop.

This man went around telling his 'friends' that he had a girl in his room, and asked the men to call. An old friend, who had known her in Russia, came to find out if the rumors that were going the rounds were true, and to his horror they were. Upon expostulating with the girl, she told him that she was doing this to help her husband, who told her it would only be for a short little while, and when he had enough money, he would start a business. Winnipeg *Telegram,* April 21st, 1910.

EXTRACTS FROM REPORT OF JUDGE ROBSON, ON
VICE CONDITIONS IN WINNIPEG

In justification of the policy of passive segregation, reference was made to another city where it was said that condition prevailed and that it was 'so successful and quiet that nobody thinks or knows anything about it.' The evidence on this enquiry shows that in this experiment the result was directly the opposite. No matter how strict were the regulations imposed on the women, they were of no effect in preventing disorderly and abominably offensive conduct in the neighborhood. One of the reasons for the keeping of a bawdy house being declared a nuisance at law is, that it endangers the public peace by drawing together dissolute and debauched persons. That such was the result was abundantly proved here.

The place selected, _____, was in the neighborhood of a considerable number of highly respected citizens. It was near the homes of residents of foreign birth. These citizens had wives and families, and most of these people, both adults and children, in going to and fro between their homes and the city, whether to their work or to school, church or market, had to pass through the area in question. Several of the male residents and two respectable women gave evidence at the enquiry. It was evident that they were people who, not pretending to any rank, were of the highest respectability and exemplary citizens. The state of affairs described by them as existing since the establishment of the segregated area was shocking. I will not use the language necessary to describe it in detail ... Such depreciation has resulted from the conditions described, that their property has become almost valueless and unsaleable ...

That such a state of things should have existed and so continued is a reproach to any civilized community. It is the indispensable duty of civil society to protect its members in the enjoyment of their rights, both of person and property.

It is impossible to say how serious is the evil influence on the surrounding community cast by the presence of these evil resorts. The example of conditions tolerated here as set before the foreign element is most pernicious. That vice should be flaunted before young children in the manner described by the residents is deplorable. Nothing could be more likely to produce the 'Juvenile Offender.'

The question now arises: What is to be done? Fifty houses together in one area of general reputation as houses of ill-fame. Their keepers known to follow that life, and many of them repeatedly convicted of illicit liquor selling. Is this state of affairs, with its accompanying nuisance as already described, to continue, subject to punishment when disorder appears, and to an occasional small fine for breach of the License Act? If not, how is it to be terminated?

From the address of the President of the Canadian Conference of Charities and Correction, 1910:

There is no prospect of immediate profit in the problems with which this assemblage has set itself to deal, and yet surely it is eminently desirable even for the material welfare of the nation that once a year we should gather together and discuss the conditions of men who have fallen, of women who are unfortunate, of children who are homeless and helpless, putting to one side the moral and sentimental phase of the question — forgetting for the moment the claims of the bad and the unfortunate upon our attention or commiseration.

It is surely the fact that every neglected child for whom a good home is found, every law-breaker restored to a good citizenship, every practical effort to lessen the awful toll in human life that we now pay through excessive and avoidable infant mortality, or the three thousand consumptives' graves that are annually filled in this Province (Ontario), every movement to improve the conditions of the poor, to clean out the slums and bring the light of cleanliness and health to places dark with filth and disease, must ultimately conduce to our material prosperity as a people. It is as true now as when Goldsmith penned the lines:

'Ill fares the land, to hastening ills a prey,
Where wealth accumulates and men decay.'

...

The whole head is sick and the whole heart faint. From the sole of the foot, even unto the head there is no soundness in it; but wounds and bruises and festering sores; they have not been closed, neither bound up, neither mollified with oil ...

When ye spread forth your hands, I will hide mine eyes from you, yea, when ye make many prayers, I will not hear; your hands are full of blood. Wash you, make you clean; put away the evil of your doings from before mine eyes; cease to do evil, learn to do well; seek judgment, relieve the oppressed, judge the fatherless, plead for the widow. Isaiah

Then shall they also answer, saying, 'Lord, when saw we thee an hungered, or athirst, or a stranger, or naked or sick, or in prison, and did not minister unto thee?' Then shall he answer saying 'Verily I say unto you, Inasmuch as ye did it not unto one of these least, ye did it not unto me.' Jesus

REFERENCES

'Responsibility for Crime'
Phillip A. Parsons. New York: Columbia University
'Diseases of Society'
C. Frank Lydston. Philadelphia: J. B. Lippincott Co.
'The Prisoner at the Bar'
Arthur Train. New York: Charles Scribner's Sons
'Guarding a Great City'
William McAdoo. New York: Harper & Brothers
'Punishment and Reformation'
Frederick H. Wines. New York: T. Y. Crowell

'The Social Evil,' Reports of Committee of Fifteen and Committee
of Fourteen, New York
Literature published by Friends' Social Purity and Abolitionist
Association, 10 Devonshire Chambers, London, E.C.
Report of Hon. Justice Taschereau, Montreal
'The Social Evil,' Recorder Weir, Montreal
Reports of Minister of Justice
Reports of Provincial Charities
Proceedings of National Conference of Charities and Correction
Proceedings of Canadian Conference of Charities and Correction

Chapter 9

Philanthropies

Charity to-day may be justice to-morrow.

Charity — old style:
>   Yet cease not to give
>   Without any regard,
>   Though the beggars be wicked
>   Thou shall have *thy* reward.

Charity — modern:
Charity may be of a kind that will transform the unfit into such as are fit to survive, and still more readily, charity — or, to use a more appropriate term, an enlightened relief policy — may alter the conditions which create the unfit.

Edward T. Devine

Not what we give, but what we share, —
For the gift without the giver is bare;
Who gives himself with his alms feeds three —
Himself, his hungering neighbor and Me.

Lowell

THE NUMBER and variety of philanthropic agencies in our cities is almost bewildering. There are state and municipal institutions of all kinds; public societies for the relief of all sorts and conditions; church and private charities innumerable and with the most extensive ramifications. Immense sums, only a part of which are recorded in Annual Reports, are contributed toward the welfare and uplift of humanity. And yet, the needs grow apace. How much of all this effort is wisely directed, and how far it is possible to relate these various activities, so as to secure the greatest efficiency are matters of the utmost importance to the entire community. First of all let us endeavor to gain a bird's-eye view of the whole field. Then with a general idea of the relation that each part bears to the other we can proceed with a more detailed study − first, a view from the city hall tower; then a tramp through the streets, from which we may poke into all kinds of crooked alleys and odd little courts.

As our cities are still young and immature, it may be well to study the charities of a more developed city. As these are based on great human needs and social conditions similar to our own, we shall soon have all these institutions represented in each of our cities. Indeed, it is astonishing how many of them we have already. Here is the Classification as used by the Charity Organization Society of New York (Charities Directory, 1910).

CLASSIFIED LIST OF THE PHILANTHROPIC, EDUCATIONAL
AND RELIGIOUS RESOURCES OF THE CITY OF NEW YORK

Class I *Care and relief of needy families in their homes*
Division
1 Relief by employment
2 Food, fuel, clothing and general relief, including
   transportation
3 Day nurseries and kindergartens
4 Fresh air charities
5 Legal aid and advice
6 Relief for national calamities
7 Relief for foreigners
8 Special relief for various classes, callings and professions
9 Nursing and care of the sick in their homes
10 Burials

Class II *Relief for destitute, neglected and delinquent children*
Division
1 Asylums, homes and cheap lodgings for children
2 Children's societies
3 Children's courts, probation work and reformatories for children

Class III *Relief in permanent and temporary homes for adults*
Division
1 Municipal, state and national homes for destitute adults
2 Private homes for adults
3 Situations with free board, also free and cheap lodgings

Class IV *Relief for the sick*
Division
1 General hospitals
2 General dispensaries
3 Special hospitals, dispensaries and associations; also homes for
   convalescents
4 Hospitals and homes for incurables
5 Women's, children's and lying-in hospitals and women's and
   children's dispensaries
6 Training schools, homes and agencies for nurses
7 Visitation of, and diet and aid for the sick in institutions
8 Medical colleges, schools and societies
9 Ambulances

Class V *Tuberculosis, prevention and relief*
Division
1 Educational and preventive agencies
2 Dispensaries (clinics)
3 Classes for intensive treatment
4 Sanatoria for incipient cases
5 Preventoria
6 Hospitals for advanced cases
7 Day camps

Class VI *Relief for the defective*
Division
1 Relief, homes, asylums, and societies for the blind

2 Relief, homes, asylums, for deaf mutes
3 Relief for cripples, including hospitals, homes and societies
4 Relief asylums and schools for insane, feeble-minded and epileptic

Class VII *Treatment of delinquent adults*
Division
1 Reformatories for men
2 Reformatories for women
3 Probation work, prison associations and societies for the
  prevention of crime

Class VIII *Preventive social work*
Division
1 Savings and loans
2 Beneficial societies
3 Education and special training
4 Improvement of social conditions
5 Settlements
6 Clubs
7 Libraries, reading-rooms and museums

Class IX *Supervisory and educational work*
Division
1 State and municipal boards and departments
2 Private associations for the improvement of state and municipal
  institutions and departments
3 Conferences of charities and correction
4 Special training in social work

Class X *Religious and moral work*
Division
1 Churches and religious congregations:
  Baptist
  Church of Christ Scientist
  Congregational
  Disciples of Christ
  Evangelical Association of North America
  German Evangelical Synod of North America
  Friends

Hebrew
Zionist Societies
Lutheran
Methodist (Epis., Prot., etc.)
Moravian
Pentecostal Churches of America
Presbyterian (also Reformed, United Presbyterian)
Protestant Episcopal (also Reformed Episcopal)
Reformed
Roman Catholic
Swedenborgian
Unitarian
Universalist
Miscellaneous churches and missions
2 Missionary publication and tract societies
3 Religious societies and orders, sisterhoods, and deaconesses, also
training schools for religious workers
4 Societies for the suppression of gambling, societies for the
promotion of temperance, religious toleration, social purity,
sabbath observance and humanity

Surely such a table is the strongest plea that could be advanced
for some kind of union which could co-relate, and in a general way
direct the activities of all these organizations. Otherwise there must
result misdirected effort, overlapping, waste and friction – in short,
chaos. Now this work of co-relating and directing is precisely the
task that has been undertaken with varying success by the Societies
known as the Charity Organization Society, or the Associated
Charities. But a consideration of this question must be reserved for
another chapter. Let us now study in some detail, though of necessity very rapidly, these various classes specified in the preceding
table. Certain institutions will be dealt with at greater length, not
because they are always more important than the others, but
because they are typical or newer and not so well known.

CLASS I   CARE AND RELIEF OF NEEDY FAMILIES IN THEIR HOMES
This class is growing in importance. At one time it was customary to
send worn-out poor people to an alms-house – the old grandfather,
perhaps, to one institution and his aged wife to another, or fatherless

children were sent to a so-called 'home' in order that their mother might work for a living. Now, it is being recognized more and more clearly that the home should, where possible, be kept together, that home ties are most potent in the formation of character, and that even from an economic standpoint the state cannot afford to have the home broken up. Hence the increasing effort to help people in their own homes, that is, in some way to supplement, perhaps only in times of special distress, the regular resources of the home.

Division 1 One of the most frequent causes of distress is *unemployment.* It may be that 'work is scarce,' or that a man loses a particular job and there is difficulty in his finding another, or that because of his poor equipment or past record no one will employ him. Now it is a comparatively easy thing to give such a man a quarter to get a meal or to send a basket of provisions to his family, but this is the most temporary relief, and, frequently repeated, may degrade an industrious man and his family to pauperism. The demand of the self-respecting unemployed is, 'We want work, not charity.' And they are right. In this world, particularly in our new land where there is so much to be done, there ought to be work for all. The difficulty is to get the man and the work together. This ought not to be left to private initiative. The state itself should institute a system of labor bureaus. Such a system has been in operation in Germany for years and is now being introduced in England. A move in this direction has recently been made in the Province of Quebec. Only thus can the labor-power of our citizens be raised to the highest efficiency. This ought not to be a matter of charity at all. Much of the trouble arises because of lack of adjustment within our social system, and this invariably falls heaviest upon those least able to bear it. As a particular class of unemployment we might mention the problem of those employed in 'Seasonal Trades.' Milliners, for instance, have long 'slack' periods. Many employees are 'laid off.' What are they to do? Or, as another example in the West, more men are needed in construction work in the summer than in the winter. Where are those who are paid off in the fall to find work during a five months' winter? The problem is not easy of solution. One thing is certain, the community that benefits by their work ought in some way to provide them a living all the year round, and *this not as a matter of charity.*

Division 2 Of course, there are instances of *distress,* and in a large city many instances, where relief is required. Accident, disease and death, ignorance and crime, bring their heavy burdens, which often weigh heaviest on the helpless or innocent. The starving must be fed, the freezing warmed, the naked clothed, the homeless housed, the whole family perhaps removed to better surroundings or to where they may have a new chance. So there are organized relief societies to minister to these needs. The danger is that these Societies may measure their usefulness by the amount of relief given. Above all things they need to keep in mind the homely proverb, 'an ounce of prevention is worth a pound of cure.'

Division 3 The fact that many mothers have so little time to give to their children and that some of them are away at work all day long, has led to the establishment of day-nurseries and free kindergartens. In the day nurseries, babies are kept for the day, for a nominal fee, while their mothers are at work. These babies often have the care of a trained nurse, they receive better food and have more wholesome surroundings than in their own homes — and yet, we cannot but feel that we ought to work for the time when the mother will be able to care for her own child, in her own home. Much the same is true of the kindergarten. Even though the true kindergarten is able to do educational work of a higher order than can be expected of the ordinary mothers, we feel that there is the danger of the home losing one of its highest functions. The home ought to be the most beautiful child's garden. Institutional training may supplement, but cannot replace, that which should be given in the home.

Division 4 Pages might be written on the value of Fresh Air Work. Not only do the children or adults receive fresh air, but also good food and healthful surroundings and a complete change, and of greater value still, good training and heaps of wholesome fun and kind friends and often an entirely new view of life. Out from the dusty streets and hot garrets go strings of puny, pale-faced children, to return in a fortnight a happy band, fresh from the woods and the fields and the beach. The pity of it that we can't bring the woods and the fields and the lakes and streams into the city! We could, too, if we would!

Division 5 Many people are too poor or too ignorant to be able to seek assistance from the law for redress for their wrongs. For this very reason they are frequently imposed on, in ways that would astound those who almost instinctively know their rights and know how to get them. Foreigners, especially, are under a great disadvantage in a land where they do not understand the language or the customs. In many cities, societies have been organized, or departments instituted to give legal advice free, or at a nominal cost, to those who would not be able to secure it through ordinary channels. The very existence of such a society is an excellent deterrent to those conscienceless rascals who prey on the helpless members of society. In passing, may we ask why the state should not make it easy for all to secure justice? This, too, is hardly a question of charity.

Division 6 Relief for national calamities is only required in emergencies, and yet some preparation ought to be made for unforeseen disasters. In this connection the valuable work of the Red Cross Society is too well known to need comment.

Division 7 Foreigners, or more broadly, immigrants, often stand in special need of help – help that we in Canada have been altogether too slow in offering. It is true that our Government Immigration Department has done excellent work in safeguarding the interests of immigrants till they are located, and even during the first years in the new land. But much more could be done. The distress in Toronto a few years ago that led to the formation of the British Welcome League illustrates the peculiarly unfavorable conditions with which immigrants must often contend.

Division 8 Soldiers and sailors, artists and clergymen, and many other improvident or poorly-paid classes are frequently provided for by special charities. National and religious organizations often care for destitute members of their own nationality or faith.

Division 9 Many sick people can be best cared for in their own homes. Chronic invalids, those who need only occasional treatment, mothers who must care for their families, ailing children, – the large number of such cases has called for district nurses who give free, or

A day in God's out-of-doors
Children of All Peoples' Mission, Winnipeg

for a small fee, the assistance that is needed. Such nurses are sometimes connected with missions and settlements. Sometimes they
work under a distinct organization. Recently the more general recognition of the necessity of preventing disease has led to placing an
emphasis on educational work. We have now nurses who, often as an
extension of the work of pure milk stations, instruct young mothers
how to care for infants; school nurses who seek to change the home
conditions that are producing defects and diseases in the children;
special nurses who instruct incipient tubercular patients in the best
methods of warding off the dread disease; hospital social service
workers who follow the discharged patients to their homes to see
that the cure is complete and that the hospital's work is not undone.
Too much attention cannot be paid to this preventive – educational
work.

Division 10 The poorest often cling tenaciously to the thought of a
'decent burial.' So various associations, chiefly religious, national or
fraternal, assist in bearing the funeral expenses of those who have
been connected with their organizations.

CLASS II   RELIEF FOR DESTITUTE, NEGLECTED AND
DELINQUENT CHILDREN
The needy child has always made a strong appeal to the sympathies
of the charitable. With the growing recognition of the importance
of the child, there has come greater effort to save him. In no department of philanthropic work have we a greater variety of agencies at
work.

Division 1 Foundling hospitals, orphanages, Children's Homes, Boys'
Homes, Girls' Homes, Homes for the Friendless, Industrial Homes
and Reformatories, are found in every city. They have their place,
but the leaders in child-caring work are learning a more excellent
way. At the Washington Conference on the Care of Dependent
Children, the keynote was *'Home life is the highest and finest product of civilization. Children should not be deprived of it except for
urgent and compelling reasons.'* The following summary of some of
the conclusions of the Conference is worthy of the most careful
consideration:
  1 *Home care.* Children of worthy parents or deserving mothers
should, as a rule, be kept with their parents at home.

2 *Preventive work.* The effort should be made to eradicate the causes of dependency, such as disease and accident, and to substitute compensation and insurance for relief.

3 *Home finding.* Homeless and neglected children, if normal, should be cared for in families, when practicable.

4 *Cottage system.* Institutions should be on the cottage plan with small units, as far as possible.

5 *Incorporation.* Agencies caring for dependent children should be incorporated on approval of a suitable state board.

6 *Inspection.* The State should inspect the work of all agencies which care for dependent children.

7 *Inspection of educational work.* Educational work of institutions and agencies caring for dependent children should be supervised by State Educational Authorities.

8 *Facts and records.* Complete histories of dependent children and their parents based upon personal investigation and supervision should be recorded for guidance of child-caring agencies.

9 *Physical care.* Every needy child should receive the best medical and surgical attention and be instructed in health and hygiene.

10 *Co-operation.* Local child-caring agencies should co-operate and establish joint bureaus of information.

Division 2 Children's Aid Societies are doing an excellent work. The following brief description of the Ontario system of caring for neglected or dependent children is issued by Mr. J. J. Kelso:

The Ontario system of child-saving, briefly explained, is one of Government supervision and direction of Children's Aid Societies, organized in connection with a central department. These Societies are formed in all the large towns and cities, and are given exceptional power of guardianship. The local work is carried on by volunteer benevolent committees, and all children received under guardianship are reported to the central office for subsequent supervision. When a child is committed to the guardianship of a Children's Aid Society, it is examined by the doctor and dentist, so that defects may be corrected without delay. If there is any serious ailment that requires more than passing treatment, the child is treated locally, or sent to the Children's Hospital, one of the best institutions of its kind in existence, located in Toronto, but accepting as free patients any dependent child in the Province. In addition, there is an orthopedic hospital, and institutions supported entirely by the Province for the care of the feeble-minded, the deaf and dumb, blind and epileptic. Not counting many children who are temporarily cared for, an average of 300 children come under the guardianship of the societies each year, and there are now over 5,000 children under supervision. These children are personally visited by experienced agents, and a change is made when circumstances necessitate such action.

Division 3 Our Reformatories are more or less under Government supervision. One of the most important developments of recent years is the establishment of Juvenile Courts. Children have too often been dealt with as hardened criminals, associated with criminals and thus themselves manufactured into criminals. Again quoting Mr. Kelso: 'The Children's Court should undoubtedly be an educational rather than a police tribunal, conducted by specially-selected persons and held in different premises from the ordinary legal courts, either as an adjunct to the school system or under the auspices of a Children's Aid Society. Its aim is not to convict young children, but to protect them even from the consequences of their own thoughtless acts, to warn and if need be to punish the tempters or corrupters of youth and so improve the environment as to effectually prevent a recurrence of the trouble.' Specially qualified and trained probation officers are, of course, indispensable.

CLASS III   RELIEF IN PERMANENT AND
TEMPORARY HOMES FOR ADULTS

Divisions 1 *and* 2 'Work' Houses, Houses of Refuge, Old Folks' Homes, under whatever name, are at present a necessity, yet generally the dread of the aged poor. Too often the 'deserving poor' have been herded with criminals or placed in institutions in which there is scant comfort. The pension system is in every way more desirable and when practicable the home should not be broken up.

Division 3 Municipal Lodging Houses, Working Girls' Homes, Men's Own Hotels, Immigrants' Shelters, Sailors' Institutes — each ministers to a particular class who are on the verge of dependency. Whether the individuals dealt with are lifted into permanent independence of sunken into confirmed pauperism, depends very largely upon the ideals and management of these institutions. A temporary shelter should never degenerate into a 'bummers' roost.'

CLASS IV   RELIEF FOR THE SICK

When Florence Nightingale began her work she had to insist that *hospitals, whatever else they do, should not make people sick.* Since that time wonderful advances have been made and our hospitals are now models of cleanliness and comfort. It is regarded as axiomatic that the poorest should receive every attention. The truth is gradually dawning upon the public that it is in the interest of the State to keep people in good health. This is leading even the hospitals into preventive work.

Specialization in medical science brings special hospitals, as for instance, orthopedic hospitals, children's hospitals, maternity hospitals, etc. Then, supplementary to the hospital, we have convalescent homes. Many patients when discharged from the hospital are not strong and have no suitable place to which to go. The convalescent home nurses them back to full strength. Ambulances should be an essential part of the hospital service, as indeed should all that ministers to the welfare of the patient. This is already the case in the best hospitals.

CLASS V   TUBERCULOSIS, PREVENTION AND RELIEF

The terrible ravages of the white plague, together with the glad tidings that it is curable and preventable, are at last being effectively brought to the attention of the public generally. (1) Anti-Tuberculosis Societies are being formed, pamphlets issued, lectures delivered, exhibits arranged. Few educational campaigns have enlisted so many helpers and these helpers from so many classes. In the treatment of the disease, many agencies have been called into existence; (2) Dispensaries where suspected cases are examined and treated; (3) Classes for intensive treatment where a few, often from the poorer districts, are given a fighting chance (open-air schools might be mentioned in this connection); (4) Sanatoria for incipient cases – often placed in the country, where there is plenty of fresh air and sunshine and wholesome food; (5) Preventoria or Fresh Air Camps for delicate and 'run-down' people; (6) Hospitals for advanced cases; (7) Day camps where those who cannot leave the city can spend the day or part of the day amid wholesome surroundings, and night camps where working-men and women may sleep in well-ventilated rooms.

Behind all these efforts, and more fundamental, is the movement to abolish the evil conditions that are breeding consumption. 'Voting down Tuberculosis' is rather a startling phrase but one that points the way to such legislative reforms as will do much to make working and living conditions more wholesome.

CLASS VI   RELIEF FOR THE DEFECTIVE

Relief for the defective is now administered largely by the Government through institutions. There are special schools for the blind and deaf mutes; homes for cripples and epileptics and feeble-minded; and asylums for the insane and incurable. Each of these has its own special problems and even here modern social science is introducing radical and far-reaching reforms.

CLASS VII   TREATMENT OF DELINQUENT ADULTS

Reformatory homes for women are found in all our larger cities. But of much greater importance than these homes are the various recent movements for radical changes in dealing with delinquents. Major H. O. Snelgrove at the Conference of Charities and Correction said that

Our existing goal system discouraged the reformable and confirmed the incorrigible. While many improvements needed to be made in that system, there were three great reforms which should be placed in the forefront of the movement; viz., statutory provision for (1) The Probation System; (2) Indeterminate Sentences; (3) The Gaol Farm. Too long have we viewed the punishment of crime from the standpoint of the offence, instead of the offender ... As officers of the law, the time had come to right-about-turn and exert their influence in the spirit of reformation, not of retaliation; of prevention, more than of punishment. Probation or parole meant the release of a person convicted of crime under suspension of sentence and under official guardianship ... The indeterminate sentence was the corollary of the probation system and should be applied after the third conviction, leaving the term limit of imprisonment to be determined after the offender had been carefully studied and scrutinized by a tribunal of criminal anthropologists. *Report,* 1908.

At the same Conference Professor Wrong, the President of the Ontario Society for the Reformation of Inebriates, called attention to the need of a radical change in the methods of dealing with drunkards. The two things specially required at the present time are longer sentences and adequate provision for treating them when under such sentence.

A notable advance has been made in Canada in the establishment of the Penal Farm Colony at Guelph and the general use of the parole system.

The following table from Hunter's *Poverty* is valuable:

Dependents and their treatment

I   ABSOLUTE DEPENDENTS

The aged	Treatment:
The children	Proper care continued as long as
The crippled (incapable of work)	may be necessary in institutions
The incurable	or elsewhere
The blind	
The deaf and dumb	
The insane	
The epileptic	
The imbecile, idiot, feeble- minded	

II   DEPENDENTS CAPABLE OF SELF-SUPPORT

The professional vagrant	Treatment:
The professional beggar	Industrial education, repression,
The morally insane	confinement for protection of
	Society

III   TEMPORARY DEPENDENTS LIKELY TO BECOME CHRONIC

The sick especially:	Treatment:
The convalescent	Complete cure in proper
The consumptive	institutions to prevent infirmity
The inebriate	of a permanent character
Those addicted to drugs, etc.	

IV   TEMPORARY DEPENDENTS

The unemployed   Treatment:
Widows with children   To supply an economic existence
                                      free from any taint of pauperism

CLASS VIII   PREVENTIVE SOCIAL WORK

Too great emphasis cannot be laid upon preventive work of all kinds.
'Better a fence round the edge of the cliff, than an ambulance down
in the valley.'

Division 1 When temptations to spend money foolishly abound on
every hand, it is necessary to encourage the thriftless and children to
deposit their pennies and as soon as possible open up a bank account. So we have such organizations as the penny banks, which
carry the banks to those who most need it, but who are least inclined to use it. Carefully conducted loan societies often perform a
valuable service in tiding a family over a time of special need.

Division 2 There are all kinds of mutual benefit organizations —
philanthropic, religious, fraternal and commercial. Our Canadian
Government Annuities system is worthy of special study, and perhaps in this connection Industrial Insurance.

Division 3 In every city a special directory is necessary to enumerate
the educational institutions. Outside of the regular work carried on
by the state, there have arisen special institutions to provide for
special needs.
    The fact is our educational system has been too narrow in its
range of subjects and has touched too restricted a circle. Only
recently have we in Canada begun to awake to the need of industrial
or technical education. Hitherto we have made little or no provision
for the needs of our immigrants and for our great industrial army.
The privileged few have been provided with higher education. The
masses after they have left the grades of the Public School have few
educational opportunities. People's Institutes, providing for higher
needs of all kinds, should, and will, form an integral part of our
educational system. Our University, School, and Church 'plants' are
capable of being used to a much greater extent than at present.

Division 4 Every city has its numerous local organizations for the improvement of social conditions. As many social needs are common to every community, there have arisen in recent years many national or international social movements. The Charity Organization Department of the Russell Sage Foundation, New York, has recently published a most valuable little pamphlet, giving information about sixty-seven of these associations.

Division 5 Jeffrey R. Brackett, of Harvard, gives the following definition of a Settlement: 'The essence of a settlement is residence, with the right frame of mind, expressed in helpful service, in a selected neighborhood.' Settlements have proved a most important factor in the life of most American cities and are now being established in Canada. Evangelia House, Toronto, has carried on its work for some years. We now have University Settlements in Toronto and Montreal, and Neighborhood Houses in Winnipeg. Settlement work will be dealt with at greater length in the next chapter.

Division 6 Social clubs are maintained in connection with many settlements and churches, and often exist as independent institutions, as, for example, the Boys' Club, Business Girls' Club, etc.

Division 7 The beneficial influence of libraries, reading-rooms, museums and art galleries can hardly be over-estimated. They ought to be accessible to all. That means that in larger cities branches ought to be established in each locality, open at all hours, and further that in some effective way they should be brought within the range of people's living. In some American cities the social or recreation centre is accomplishing much along this line.

CLASS IX   SUPERVISORY AND EDUCATIONAL WORK

Division 1 Every intelligent citizen should know the State (that is, with us, Federal or Provincial) and municipal boards and departments.

Division 2 Municipal leagues and city clubs and reform associations are unfortunately at this stage of our development almost a necessity.

The public must be educated and the officials spurred on by private organizations.

Division 3 In Canada we have a so-called Canadian Conference of Charities and Corrections, which unfortunately is largely confined to the Province of Ontario.

Division 4 So far, notwithstanding its great importance, we have no institution in Canada which gives special training for social work. Several fine schools have been established in the United States, in which practical instruction is given to those preparing for what has been termed: 'The New Profession.'

CLASS X   RELIGIOUS AND MORAL WORK

Information concerning the local churches and Missions ought to be available in every city. The work of Missionary Societies and Deaconesses and Bible Training Schools is well known. The Reports of Temperance Societies, the Lord's Day Alliance and similar organizations for special objects should be carefully consulted.

We give a list (slightly modified for Canada) of the social facts with reference to his own city or town that each student in the Charity Organization Institute of the New York School of Philanthropy has been asked to bring to the school.

I *Population*

(a) Population at last census.

(b) Your estimate of the increase which the forthcoming census will show.

(c) What foreign elements did the last census show and in what proportion for each nationality?

(d) Will there be any marked changes in these proportions in the 1911 census?

(e) What forces are Canadianizing your foreign groups?

II *Location*

What geographical or climatic conditions are, in your opinion, important factors in the social situation?

III *Industries*

(a) What is the total per capita wealth?

Sharing with 'our neighbors'
Christmas at All Peoples' Mission, Winnipeg

(b) What are the leading industries?

(c) What relation do these have to your poverty problem?

(d) What are the wages in these industries for unskilled labor and what proportion of those employed are unskilled?

(e) To what extent are these industries seasonal?

(f) What is the relative proportion of women employed?

(g) Of children employed?

(h) In what proportion are the proprietors or chief corporation officers of large industrial plants residents and not residents?

IV *Health*

(a) What are the powers of the Board of Health?

(b) What is the death rate?

(c) What is the death rate for children under one year? Or for those under five, if the other figure is not obtainable?

(d) What is the tuberculosis death rate?

(e) What are the ordinances regulating sewerage connection and water supply?

(f) What is the tuberculosis situation?

(g) What is the housing situation?

V *Conditions surrounding children*

(a) What are the state laws governing school attendance and child labor, and how well are these enforced?

(b) What are the types of amusement for the young? Describe the playground situation.

(c) How are juvenile delinquents dealt with?

(d) Has any progress been made in the socialization of the Public School?

VI *Charities*

(a) What social tasks has private charity undertaken in your community?

(b) Describe the local relief situation, both public and private.

(c) What definite relations do your charities have to one another?

(d) What is the attitude of your commercial bodies toward social work?

(e) What is the attitude of the churches?

(f) Of the newspapers?

(g) Of the City officials?

REFERENCES

'The Survey'
A Journal of Constructive Philanthropy, 105 East 22nd St.,
New York
'Misery and its Causes' and 'The Principles of Relief'
Edward T. Devine. New York: The Macmillan Co.
'Friendly Visiting Among the Poor' — 'The Good Neighbor in the
Modern City'
Mary E. Richmond. Philadelphia: J. B. Lippincott Co.
'Treatment of Juvenile Delinquents'
Richard Ray Perkins. Chicago: University of Chicago
'New Ideals in Healing'
Ray Stannard Baker. New York: Frederick A. Stokes Co.
'Social Service and the Art of Healing'
Richard C. Cabot, M.D. New York: Moffat, Yard & Co.
'Tuberculosis'
L. A. Knopf. New York: Moffat, Yard & Co.
'Beginnings in Industrial Education'
Paul H. Hanus. Boston: Houghton, Mifflin Co.
Reports of Societies and Institutions
'Inter-relation of Social Movements' (pamphlet)
Charity Organization Dept., Russell Sage Foundation, 105 East
22nd St., New York

Chapter 10

Social service

There is no secular.

Graham Taylor

Men think there are circumstances when one may deal with human beings without love, and there are no such circumstances. One may deal with things without love; one may cut down trees, make bricks, hammer iron, without love, but you cannot deal with men without love.

Tolstoi

We must reascend to the conception of humanity in order to ascertain the secret rule and law of life of the individual, of man.

Jos. Mazzini

One Christian city, one city in any part of the earth, whose citizens, from the greatest to the humblest, lived to the spirit of Christ, where religion had overflowed the churches, and passed into the streets, inundating every house and workshop and permeating the whole social and commercial life — one such Christian city would seal the redemption of the world.

Henry Drummond, in *A City without a Church*

SOCIAL SERVICE is no new thing. Individuals, churches, charitable institutions, public bodies of all kinds, have been serving the community in a countless variety of ways. But in recent years a new viewpoint has been attained, new types of work developed and a new enthusiasm evoked. It is difficult to define the limits of this new-spirit movement, or to state its characteristics. But its presence is being recognized and its various manifestations have been grouped under the name Social Service. This modern impulse can be traced to no one individual or organization. It reveals itself in men of the most diverse creeds. It is expressing itself in a great variety of activities, some new, some old. It is gradually permeating and leaving our social life and is destined to transform our institutions. It is our *zeitgeist,* going forth conquering and to conquer.

To give an account of the various forms of social service would manifestly be to write a history of social institutions. Our churches and charities, our schools and universities, our industrial and commercial enterprises, the professions, the press — all these have a well-recognized place and value. But the needs of the city are calling forth fresh efforts. The older institutions are gradually adapting themselves to the altered environment, and many new organizations are being created to meet the new conditions. We propose to call attention to several of the more recent and, in this country, less well-known types of social service. The great guiding principles of these are common to the best development in all the 'old line' institutions.

In a small community it is easy to give relief to the occasional needy family. There exists a personal relationship which largely precludes imposition, and which goes far in encouraging thrift. But in the city the situation is quite changed. The well-to-do are separated from their less fortunate neighbors by distance and by social cleavages of many kinds. The very numbers make personal knowledge and sympathy almost an impossibility. How to get the man who needs help into touch with the man who can help is the problem. With no system there has been on the one hand much indiscriminate and harmful almsgiving, and, on the other hand, much needless misery, and, worse than all, no earnest attempt to cope with underlying evils.

Let me illustrate. A few weeks ago I was sitting in the office of a kindly, Christian gentleman. A sturdy but unkempt fellow opened the door, proffering boot laces – an occupation generally recognized as a thinly-veiled form of begging. The gentleman produced a quarter. 'There, take that,' he said, 'it's all I have for you. Keep the laces. Good morning.' Well, that was the easiest way, but was it the best – the right?

The gentleman was kindly, he couldn't bear to 'turn down' a poor fellow who was 'down and out.' But let us follow our man. Ten to one he is a professional impostor, who ought to be dealt with most severely by the law. But if this is the first time he has begged, a new light has come to him – the secret of making 'easy money.' He probably tries the next office; it is to be hoped that he will not get another push on the downward path. What does he do with his quarter? Probably drinks it. If he should go and buy a good meal, how much better off is he? Where will he get the next meal? Where will he sleep? Nothing has been done to set the poor fellow on his feet again or to remove the conditions that are driving him and hundreds more to pauperism and moral ruin.

What should have been done? Ideally, perhaps, the kindly gentleman should have gained the confidence of his visitor; found out his story, verified it by following the man to his home or former occupation, then treated him as he would his own unfortunate brother under similar circumstances. If possible he should have secured work for him, encouraged him and helped him to fight his battles.

But in practice this would be almost impossible. So there has been gradually evolved an organization for meeting such a situation. The generally approved method of dealing with our boot-laces vendor is for the kindly gentleman and all other well-disposed people to absolutely refuse to give him any 'charity' at the door. Instead a card should be given him, directing him to the office of the Charity Organization Society. If he is not an impostor, he will present this introduction. The specially-trained and experienced secretary will investigate the case, provide him with meals on condition that he is willing to work, then find him a permanent situation. If beggars are numerous, if work is scarce, if intemperance is prevalent, these evils will be forced home on the secretary and the members of the Charity Organization Society, who will then make some determined and intelligent effort to eradicate them. The kindly gentleman is, of course, expected to support the organization and to *give his personal services in carrying on the Society's work.* Which method is the better?

In Canada, probably the best organized and most efficient Society of this kind is the Associated Charities of Winnipeg. In order to illustrate this class of work, we take the liberty of quoting freely from the introductory report of the General Secretary, Mr. J. H. T. Falk.

The Associated Charities is a social agency, working for the betterment of individuals and conditions in the municipality of Winnipeg. The Society has now been actively at work for one year, and its existence has been fully justified by the results obtained.

The Society acts in a three-fold capacity: Firstly, to co-ordinate the work of all other Charities in the city, acting as their clearing house; secondly, as a bureau of investigation for relief cases, and lastly, as a relief-giving agency. Private individuals and those holding a semi-official capacity have been relieved of the responsibility of giving or refusing assistance, and have referred applicants for investigation by the Society's especially trained agents.

In its relief work the sequence of efforts is to find means by which families may help themselves, or relatives who should assist, or other organizations on whom the applicant for relief has some reasonable claims, and only as a last resource to supply relief direct from the Society's funds; this fact accounts for the comparatively large expenditures on salaries and office expenses when compared with the actual cost of material relief given.

The public must not lose sight of the fact that main work of the Associated Charities is to advise, counsel and direct those who, by misfortune or abuse of fortune, find themselves in need of assistance ...

We are well aware that to some people the acme of charity is to give away without enquiry, considering that the amount of good done is in direct proportion to the amount of relief given; to such persons scientific charity, involving the most careful investigation of the circumstances of the applicant for relief, a systematic recordance of the facts, and an intelligent consideration of the conditions which led to dependency, is not only distasteful, but also criticized as hard-hearted and expensive, necessitating as it does the payment of salaries which will engage employees, capable of undertaking such careful investigations. To these persons we would emphasize the quotation on the cover of the report, 'Charity, chief of the virtues, ceases to be even a virtue, when wise order is missing from it.'

So exact is the simile between the giving of medical and the giving of charitable relief, that we do not hesitate to compare them, A person is sick, he calls in the doctor, who 'investigates' his case, asking many questions and making mental, and perhaps written, record of the answers and his own deductions therefrom. He then prescribes the medicine, which is to 'relieve' the patient. Is he content to remain away until the 'relief' is finished? No, he visits constantly to see that the treatment is adhered to and not abused, that is, to see that the patient is helping himself to get well; possibly he changes the form of 'relief' and thus continues until the patient is independent once more. And so it is with the 'disease' of poverty, and even the strongest opponent of scientific and organized charity must now bow to the admission of the fact that poverty is a disease.

If the Doctor of Charity fails to 'diagnose' his case correctly; if after one fleeting visit, having 'prescribed' the 'medicine' of wood and groceries, he leaves the patient to himself until the 'medicine' is finished, without close supervision to prevent the abuse of his treatment, then in nine cases out of ten the patient will not recover, but will decline to a more hopeless state of the disease of poverty, by which time he is termed 'pauperized' and beyond cure.

We hope this statement will incite careful thought of the subject of charity and poverty; for those who would go further into it comes the question, who are to be these Doctors of Charity? They must be fully trained persons having an intimate knowledge of all local institutions for the care of different classes of persons, of hospitals, free dispensaries, of employers of labor, of laws respecting health, child labor, employers' liability, non-support, desertion, and other matters.

These salaried social doctors have only sufficient time to diagnose the cases as they occur, and to form a plan of treatment, which if followed, will lead to the permanent improvement desired. This improvement will not be attained unless volunteer friendly visitors can be secured, who, taking a personal interest in the families allotted to them, will superintend the treatment with regular friendly visits.

Such volunteers must be drawn from the families of citizens,

who, owing a debt to the community for the good fortune which
God has bestowed in blessing them with a good education and the
example of a happy, well-ordered home life, should repay that debt
in free service, giving of the fruits of their education to those to
whom it has been denied. In Germany, by the Elberfeld System of
Relief, all capable citizens must serve three years as 'Armenpfleger'
volunteer helpers. It has been said that the 'Armenpfleger' begin by
having the care 'of' a family and end by caring 'for' the family, and
so it must be here in Winnipeg. We do not want it to be the 'fashion'
to become a volunteer worker to the Associated Charities; the duty
once undertaken must be as sacred as it would be, were the 'helper'
caring for his or her own family.

Criticism has constantly been levelled at organized charities for
not obtaining the co-operation of the Churches. The criticism is
justified where no attempt has been made to effect that co-
operation. In Winnipeg the Associated Charities is not only anxious
to obtain it, but feels that without it effective charity will be impossible. In the churches we find already existent the perfect organization from which to recruit the ranks of volunteers. At this time
when missionary work of all kinds is receiving fresh encouragement
and support, it should not be difficult to attract 'home missionaries.'
Perhaps it is not generally recognized, and yet it is none the less a
fact, that not one family in one hundred needing relief will be found
to be 'church-going,' much less church members. Was there ever a
more obvious, glorious opportunity for the churches to bring into
the fold the lost sheep of the community? ...

We believe:

1 Pauperism can be eliminated.

2 Poverty is curable.

3 Both pauperism and poverty can be prevented.

4 In order to eliminate the one, cure the other, and prevent both,
individual sentimentality must make way for enlightened sympathy
and co-operative social effort.

5 Attempts to treat a poverty-sick man without finding out the
cause of his poverty are like unto the efforts put forth to cure a
fever-stricken patient without diagnosis. The one is the method of
the charity quack, the other the method of the medical quack. Both
cause mischief. There is no cure in either instance.

6 On account of the complicated neighborhood, industrial, social

MAP OF THE HEART OF WINNIPEG

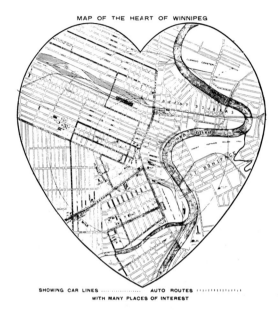

SHOWING CAR LINES .... AUTO ROUTES ||||||||||||||||
WITH MANY PLACES OF INTEREST

THE ASSOCIATED CHARITIES.

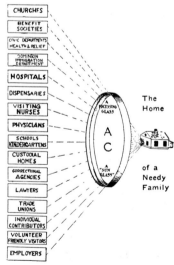

A FOCUSSING GLASS—A SUN GLASS.

and economic conditions in a large city, special knowledge and training and special personal fitness are called for in those who would
deal effectively with human wreckage.

7 Careful attention to the condition of the children of the poor is
absolutely necessary in the effort to reduce the volume of future
poverty.

8 While scrutiny of the personal causes of poverty is important,
still without the examination and remedying of social and economic
causes little advance will be made in the campaign against misery,
want, disease and death.

9 Lack of co-operation among churches, charities, institutions
and charitable individuals who deal with the poor spells M-O-B —
and leads to M-O-B methods and no results.

10 Winnipeg can have just as much beggary, poverty and pauperism as she is willing to pay for and can have just as much freedom
from beggary, poverty and pauperism as she is willing to work for!

The following article especially prepared by Mr. J. Blaine Gwin
(Head Relief Agent, Associated Charities, Winnipeg), shows just how
this Society co-operates with the other charitable organizations of
the city:

Effective co-operation must include not only the co-operation of all
charitable societies and churches, but also co-operation between the
charitable societies and the municipal, Dominion and Provincial
officials, as well as with individual citizens of the city who are
interested in charitable work.

There are three kinds of co-operation: First, a co-operation for the
giving of material relief; second, a co-operation by refraining from
giving material relief; and third, a co-operation in other ways than
the giving of material relief, such as in visiting, nursing, providing a
home for the children and in securing advice and protection for all
the different members of the family.

We have been enabled to secure this co-operation in Winnipeg
in two ways: First, by means of the Joint Registration Bureau,
located at the offices of the Associated Charities. Most of the other
societies send in weekly a list of the families that they have been in
touch with during the week; this list includes enough about each
family for the purpose of identification, and also a statement as to

the number of visits made, and any relief that may have been given. This list is kept on file and is not accessible to the general public, but can be seen at any time by those who are interested in any of the families included in that list; second, by means of a weekly Case Conference held also at the offices of the Associated Charities. This conference is composed of representative workers from most of the other organizations in Winnipeg, and also includes representatives from many of the churches and private individuals who may be interested in some family. At the conference the workers of the Associated Charities, who are the investigators for the conference, bring up for discussion the situation in some family presenting difficult problems. It often happens, though, that other members of the conference will also present the name of some family. Besides the information secured through the investigation made by the agents of the Associated Charities, many of the other members present will also know of that family through their work, and will give what information they have. After a free discussion, a decision is generally arrived at. This decision will include work to be done, not only by the agents of the Associated Charities, but by many of the other members of the conference.

I can, perhaps, illustrate this better by showing just what was done for two families which came up for discussion at conference. It must be remembered, though, that everything that is disclosed about the families at conference is strictly confidential, and is given only because it may be used to help the family more effectively.

1 *Icelandic family, W.* Consisted of the father, who was almost blind, the crippled mother and eight children, the oldest of whom was eighteen years and the youngest four. In order to assist this family it was necessary to have the co-operation of the clergy, the city officials, the probation officers of the Juvenile Court, the nurse from the nursing mission and the agents of the Associated Charities.

The nurse from the mission was first called upon to visit the family, to nurse the sick mother; she found them living in a very small shack, almost surrounded by water. The inside of the house was extremely filthy and crowded; she reported at once to the Health Department, who had already known of the condition of the house and were unable to force the family to move out because they were not, at that time, able to provide a better place. The Health Department then reported the matter to the Associated Charities, asking for assistance to force the family to vacate the house.

A short time before this, one of the younger boys had been before the Juvenile Court because his father could not control him, and a clergyman had been appointed as a voluntary probation officer, to take an interest in the boy; the family had also been helped for a considerable time by the City Relief Department.

When this case was brought up at conference, there were present the clergyman, the nurse, the head of the City Relief Department, the agent who had made the investigation for the Associated Charities, and the minister from the Icelandic Church who had acted as interpreter, besides the other members who had not been in touch with the family. In addition to this the Health Department had been communicated with, and they had expressed themselves as to what they thought should be done.

First, it was decided to assist the family to move into a better house and to pay their rent until they could pay it themselves. Second, to appoint as a friendly visitor the Icelandic minister, to secure work for the oldest boy, who was inclined to be indolent, and to attempt to keep him steadily at work through the aid of the friendly visitor. The furniture for the new house was to be supplied by the Associated Charities and the Icelandic Church, as the furniture they had was too filthy to take with them; the rent for the first month was to be paid by the Associated Charities and for the second month by the Icelandic Church.

The Health Department were notified of the decision, and in a short time were enabled to force the family to vacate, as they were able to explain to the magistrate that another house had been provided for them to move into.

They moved five months ago and for the past three months have not only been able to pay their own rent, $15.00 a month, but have paid $10.00 a month on a lot which they bought, and on which they intend to build as soon as possible. The two older boys are working regularly, and the younger boy, who had been before the Juvenile Court, has been sent to the Reform School. As their former church is now too far away, a minister of the Church of England has been interested and has gotten three of the children into his Sunday School, and hopes soon to get the others to attend.

Each of the organizations, despite their best efforts for the good of this family, would have been powerless to effect any lasting good without the active co-operation of all the others.

2 *English family, H.* This family was referred to the Associated Charities by the City Relief Department, who had been assisting them for several years. We found, by referring to our index records, that they were known by members of the Deaconess' Home, by the City Relief Department, and by the nursing mission and All Peoples' Mission.

The family consisted of the father, who was supposed to be tubercular, the mother who was sick, a girl aged 18, two boys aged 16 and 14, all of whom were working, and five smaller children. The total income of the family was $11.50 a week, but the boys were very unreliable and were frequently being discharged, and often out of work. Mr. H., who was not working, was known by five different physicians; he would go to one physician and soon become dissatisfied, and then go to another. They had all become discouraged with him, as he did not stay long enough with them for them to see just what the trouble was, and they were unwilling to do anything for him. The relatives of the family, who had before that time helped them, had decided that Mr. H. was not sick, but only lazy, and would do nothing further.

When the case was brought up at conference, it was found that they had been receiving assistance from almost all the other organizations mentioned, and that they all felt that so far no real good had been accomplished. It was decided at conference to make them a regular allowance of $3.00 a week, fuel and necessary clothing, for the present; to insist on the mother remaining at home, as she had spoken of going out to work; to have the man examined by a competent physician, and, if necessary, have a consultation of physicians; to appoint as friendly visitor a deaconess from All Peoples' Mission, who was to make a special effort to keep the boys at work; all relief from other sources, with the exception of the amount mentioned, was to be stopped, and the family were to be given to understand that the continuance of this relief would depend on the efforts they made to do what the conference wished.

After considerable trouble and after communicating with all the physicians who had previously known the family, one was appointed to make a careful examination of Mr. H., so as to determine definitely what his trouble was, so an attempt could be made to cure him. This physician examined him and called into consultation two other

physicians, who had previously known Mr. H. It was decided that
Mr. H. was not tubercular, but that he had dilatation of the stomach
and gastritis, and that if he would be operated upon he could be
cured in six weeks. Mr. H. refused to submit to the operation and
wanted to go to another physician. When he found that as he had no
money to pay a physician himself, and that no other doctor would
be secured for him, but that he must abide by the decision of this
one, he claimed to be feeling much better and wanted to work. The
conference decided that next week to let him do some light work if
he desired, and a position was secured, working on the streets for the
City, through the assistance of the City Relief Department. He was
required to work only a half day at a time.

In the meantime better food was secured for Mrs. H. and she
became stronger and better contented; the boys were interested in
their work and finally settled down to steady positions. Mr. H.
complained of sickness again, but would not submit to an operation,
and tried to get some other physicians to give him another examination. but they refused; he went back to his work again. Since that
time, although his health is only fair, he is working steadily, and the
income of the family has been sufficient so that the weekly allowance and all other aid has been stopped. The situation is still
somewhat unsatisfactory as Mr. H. will never be strong until he has
had an operation, but they have been placed in an independent
position in a few months through the active co-operation of the
Charities; harm and demoralization was the only thing that had been
accomplished previously by these societies, working separately and
at cross purposes.

It would be almost impossible to find among our records the
history of any family in which there has not been an active co-
operation with at least one society. Many of them will show that
almost every society in the city has worked with the Associated
Charities for the betterment of the family.

Co-operation does not lessen the work of the organization, but
increases it. It shows them that there are many things to be done,
which they had not thought of before. But, more important, it gives
each of them an opportunity to develop their own special work and
to do in an effective manner the one thing that they are best fitted
to do.

In the American cities, with their mixed population, their rapid industrial development, their corrupt politics, and the general apathy of the public, the social settlements have been one of the foremost agencies in bringing about better conditions. They have broken down prejudices, swept away abuses, maintained a campaign of publicity and secured and enforced reform legislation.

The 'Settlement' is simply a group of persons who make their home in a poor district and try to act the part of good neighbors. They make the interests of the neighborhood their own. They gain the confidence of the people of the district and seek to secure for them what they most value in their own lives. Often the 'Residents' of a settlement make a living at their ordinary occupations, and simply spend their evenings in social or educational work among their neighbors.

In *The Burden of the City*, Miss Isabella Horton gives a sympathetic account of the work at Hull House, with which she was so familiar:

Hull House, founded and still carried on by Miss Addams, and recognized as the most complete and effectively managed institution of its kind in existence, may be taken as the example and type of the purely social settlement in its most highly developed form. It is situated in one of the worst quarters of Chicago, on Halsted Street, which is said to be the longest city thoroughfare in the world. Running the entire length of the city, beginning and ending in open stretches of country, its course for a while is between handsome residences with shaded walks and well-kept lawns, but soon it plunges into the strenuous life of the down-town district. The tiny grass patches flanking the sidewalks disappear. Shops, factories and saloons multiply. The din and roar of traffic stuns the ear; the air grows thick and smoky, the sidewalk is filled with people. The street becomes a maze of delivery wagons, dump carts, and vehicles of all descriptions, loaded with every conceivable kind of wares. Street cars plunge through at intervals of two or three minutes, filled morning and evening with a dense mass of humanity, hanging to straps inside and clinging to steps and railing outside, and packing every available inch of space. Between the larger stores and factories are huddled cheap groceries, sordid fancy shops, and an occasional

dwelling-house, smoke-blackened and dingy. The display of wares on
the street is most unsavory. Narrow streets and alleys branching off
on either side afford vistas of wretchedness. There are sooty tenements, tumble-down sheds and foul stables. Dirty children, in all
sorts of demi-toilet, swarm everywhere. They occupy the stairways,
hang over the window-sills, and carry on their games on the sidewalk
in utter disregard of the public gaze, and, truth to tell, the public
hurries on its way with as little attention for them.

The names over the shop doors grow portentous. Masalis Mart-
jinkis, Isadore Yesariwitch, Slephe & Jaffe, and Demetrios
Manussopoulis advertise their wares to the public and solicit patronage. Interspersed with these are signs in the unknown characters of
the Hebrew or Yiddish.

But presently, through an archway, one sees a flash of green grass
and trees. A few steps and you are standing before the porticoed
front of an old but dignified-looking red brick house, set well back
from the sidewalk. The little court thus formed is well paved and
clean, and benches invite to rest. You recognize instinctively that
this is not a house thrown together by the exigencies of trade, but
that it is a place with a history and a purpose. This is Hull House, and
around it is crowded one of the most cosmopolitan populations
under the sun. Italians, Greeks, Russians, Poles, Germans, Jews,
Bohemians and a score of other races to the number of 60,000,
swarm within the area of a few blocks, and to all this building opens
its doors of welcome.

Around the central building have grown up half a block of connected buildings. Departments of work have been added as their
need became apparent. There is the 'Jane Club,' a co-operative
boarding-house for working girls and women; there is a picturesque
restaurant or coffee-house copied from an old English inn, with low,
dark rafters and diamond-paned windows, where for a moderate
price you can be served with a wholesome luncheon in irreproach-
able style. There is the 'Children's House' with its kindergarten and
day nursery. A playground was secured for the children by having
half a dozen old tenements torn away and occupying the space with
swings, summer-houses, teeters and sand piles. There is a large gymnasium, and an art gallery with studios for art classes; there are
music rooms, a library and reading-rooms. Everywhere there is
evidence of cultivated taste. Furniture is handsome and genuine; no
cheap or tawdry imitations are permitted. On the walls hang

photographs from the masters of art. Friezes from the Parthenon, casts from Phidias and Praxiteles decorate halls and stairways. Even the children's rooms are furnished with choice pictures and casts from Della Robbia and Donatello, and the wee tots climb upon chairs to kiss the immortal mother and child from Raphael. 'Much is gained,' says Miss Addams, 'if one can begin in a very little child to make a truly beautiful thing truly beloved.'

A simple list of the multitudinous activities constantly going on in these capacious buildings would fill pages of the present volume. They touch every department of art, travel, industry, literature and social progress. Miss Addams has the rare faculty of gathering around her men and women of leadership who carry out their own plans, untrammelled, save by the predominant idea of mutual good. About twenty persons are usually in residence. The governing power is vested in a simple organization among these. A hundred more come weekly to the settlement as lectures, teachers, leaders of clubs, etc. It is estimated that two thousand people of the neighborhood come every week to share the benefits of the institution.

Hull House has come to be a recognized influence in social and labor circles, looking out for the interests of the laboring classes, yet often taking a conservative position and aiming to secure justice to all concerned. It is also a factor to be reckoned with in the politics of the ward. More than one disreputable 'Boodler' has owed his defeat at the polls to the opposition of Hull House residents. While it enjoys the confidence of labor unions, it has at least the wholesome respect of the capitalist class. Miss Addams is a recognized leader of the great onward sweep of thought in the direction of social righteousness. In its immediate neighborhood Hull House has produced cleaner streets, better sanitary conditions, better housing and better lighting. It has had a marked influence in purifying civic politics and is a 'power house' of social and intellectual life and light, as well as a school of ethical culture to a wide coterie of men and women.

Miss Addams has given us her own ideals in *Twenty Years at Hull House:*

The Settlement, then, is an experimental effort to aid in the solution of the social and industrial problems which are engendered by the

modern conditions of life in a great city. It insists that these problems are not confined to any one portion of the city. It is an attempt
to relieve at the same time the over-accumulation at one end of
society and the destitution at the other; but it assumes that this
over-accumulation and destitution is most sorely felt in the things
that pertain to social and educational advantages. From its very
nature it can stand for no political or social propaganda. It must in a
sense give the warm welcome of an inn to all such propaganda, if
perchance one of them be found an angel. The one thing to be
dreaded in the Settlement is, that it lose its flexibility, its power of
quick adaptation, its readiness to change its methods as its environment may demand. It must be open to conviction and must have a
deep and abiding sense of tolerance. It must be hospitable and ready
for experiment. It should demand from its residents a scientific
patience in the accumulation of facts and the steady holding of their
sympathies as one of the best instruments for that accumulation. It
must be grounded in a philosophy whose foundation is on the
solidarity of the human race, a philosophy which will not waver
when the race happens to be represented by a drunken woman or an
idiot boy. Its residents must be emptied of all conceit of opinion and
all self-assertion, and ready to arouse and interpret the public
opinion of their neighborhood. They must be content to live quietly
side by side with their neighbors until they grow into a sense of
relationship and mutual interests. Their neighbors are held apart by
differences of race and language which the residents can more easily
overcome. They are bound to see the needs of their neighborhood as
a whole, to furnish data for legislation, and to use their influence to
secure it. In short, residents are pledged to devote themselves to the
duties of good citizenship, which too largely lie dormant in every
neighborhood given over to industrialism. They are bound to regard
the entire life of their city as organic, to make an effort to unify it
and to protest against its over-differentiation.

In more than one settlement the following little poem has been
posted as expressing the spirit of the house:

THE HOUSE BY THE SIDE OF THE ROAD
By Sam Walter Foss
    There are hermit souls that live withdrawn
    In the peace of their self-content;

There are souls, like stars, that dwell apart,
In a fellowless firmament;
There are pioneer souls that blaze their paths
Where highways never ran;
But let me live by the side of the road
And be a friend to man.

Let me live in a house by the side of the road
Where the race of men go by —
The men who are good and the men who are bad,
As good and as bad as I.
I would not sit in the scorner's seat,
Or hurl the cynic's ban;
Let me live in a house by the side of the road
And be a friend to man.

I see from my house by the side of the road,
By the side of the highway of life,
The men who press with the ardor of hope,
The men who are faint with the strife.
But I turn not away from their smiles nor their tears —
Both parts of an infinite plan —
Let me live in my house by the side of the road
And be a friend to man.

I know there are brook-gladdened meadows ahead
And mountains of wearisome height;
That the road passes on through the long afternoon
And stretches away to the night,
But still I rejoice when the travellers rejoice,
And weep with the strangers that moan,
Nor live in my house by the side of the road
Like a man who dwells alone.

Let me live in a house by the side of the road
Where the race of men go by —
They are good, they are bad, they are weak, they are strong,
Wise, foolish — so am I.
Then why should I sit in the scorner's seat,

Or hurl the cynic's ban? —
Let me live in my house by the side of the road
And be a friend to man.

The ordinary social work of the local churches is well known and its value appreciated by all. It is not so generally recognized that these local churches are generators of much of the moral earnestness and devoted service that finds its expression outside the church walls, and beyond the range of the regular church activities. While we must confine ourselves here to a few forms of social service directly undertaken by the church, we do not for a moment lose sight of or underestimate what in contrast is often called 'ordinary' church work. In the city, two more or less clearly distinguished types of work have developed — 'The Institutional Church' and 'The Mission.'

'An Institutional Church,' Says Edward Judson, 'is an organized body of Christian believers, who finding themselves in a hard and uncongenial social environment, supplement the ordinary methods of the gospel, such as preaching, prayer-meetings, Sunday school and pastoral visitation, by a system of organized kindness, a *congeries* of institutions, which by touching people on physical, social and intellectual sides will conciliate them and draw them within reach of the gospel. The local church under the pressure of adverse environment tends to institutionalize.'

Most of our down-town churches, and many of our suburban churches, are beginning to introduce institutional features. These vary from a club room opened one or two nights a week to well-equipped buildings in which are carried on almost numberless activities. The great English Missions, while emphasizing the evangelistic side of the work, are splendid examples of institutional churches. The most highly developed organization on this side of the water is Saint Bartholomew's Episcopal Church, New York. The Parish House resembles a great office block. The visitor takes the elevator and goes up and up, past offices and class rooms and club rooms of every description, till he is quite confused by the extent and complexity of it all.

The following table of statistics from the Report of 1910 will give some idea of the possible development of an institutional church:

STATISTICS

Clergy	7	Secretaries and clerks	11
Deaconesses	2	Pianists	7
Lay reader	1	Custodians	2
Organists	3	Telephone operators	2
Assistant organists	4	Printers	4
Choir members	69	Painter	1
Physicians	1	Carpenters	2
Parish visitors	4	Watchman	1
Matrons	2	Janitor	1
Dentists	1	Engineers, firemen, etc.	5
Druggists	1	Laundresses	5
Nurses	6	Porters and cleaners	19
Housekeeper and assistants	3	Gardeners	3
Superintendent and assistants	6	Farm hands	3
Kindergartners	9	Cooks and helpers	5
Attendants (kindergarten)	2	Waitresses	3
Instructors and teachers in		Chambermaids	4
clubs	46	Useful men	4
Librarians	3	Physical directors	2
Sextons and assistants	5		
		Total	259

VOLUNTEERS

Wardens and Vestry, St. Bartholomew's Church	11
Wardens and Vestry, Swedish Chapel	8
Advisory Board, German Congregation	12
Lay workers, Chinese Guild	11
Ushers	12
Officers and teachers, Sunday Schools	118
Officers and teachers, Industrial School	9
Officers of Societies, St. Bartholomew's Church	23
Physicians, St. Bartholomew's Clinic	52
Choirs, St. Bartholomew's Parish House, etc.	42
Workers in Various Societies and Clubs	174
Total	472

'The Mission' is, on this continent, generally established in a poor section of the city by some wealthy church or group of churches. Sometimes it is designed to reach a special class, as for instance, Rescue Missions, the Italian or Jewish Missions. Some Missions are almost exclusively evangelistic, others introduce many institutional features. Too often, Missions do not receive adequate financial or moral support. A second-rate minister and an overburdened deaconess are placed in a shabby little hall and supplied with a few cast-off hymn books and old clothes, and are expected to evangelize and uplift a neglected community. Fortunately there are at least a few Missions in Canada that are well equipped and supported. The work they have accomplished at least shows something of the magnitude of the problem.

Rev. S. W. Dean, Superintendent of the Toronto City and Fred Victor Mission, has very kindly contributed the following on 'The Needs and Nature of our Mission Ministries':

1 Let me speak of the unchurched masses in Toronto. We have been well called the City of Churches. The total number of all denominations is 277, and their seating capacity, possibly, 150,000. A Southern visitor described our moral life as being like unto a Sunday school, compared with his town. But this does not meet the need of our people. Our population is 340,000, at least, and it is increasing at the rate of about seven per cent. per annum, whilst our church accommodation is not progressing faster than two or four per cent. What becomes of the balance? Time was when we felt that easily three-quarters of our people were represented in our churches. But now it is doubtful if more than one-half are.

2 The victims of personal intemperance are the second class named. Toronto may have a favorable record before the world, in this respect. Compared with San Francisco, we have 110 licenses, while that city, with about one-fifth more population, has 2,500 saloons. Buffalo, with similar population, has about 1,200, and Detroit has about 1,650. It may seem a favorable state of things that not more than 10,132 arrests and apprehensions for drunkenness were made in our city last year, but that would mean one out of every thirty-five of our population, and if that one were your father, or son, or husband, or wife, it would be as bad as though the whole city were dissipated. Toronto may not have as many drinking

saloons as some cities, but she has many men who drink as much, fall as fast and sink as low as the victims of drink in any other city in the world. The shambling, nerveless creatures which the sons of good homes become is a crime which must cry aloud to high heaven, and is enough to make the angels weep. But the drunkard's broken-hearted wife, his diseased, deformed, emaciated, needy children, reveal a crime which calls for speedy annihilation of the contributing traffic by the sane and strong.

3 Social vice undoubtedly exists in Toronto, yet neither by toleration of the authorities nor consent of the general public. Only those very intimate with our streets and with the habits of our wayward could discover its presence. Vigorously has this vice been pursued by the Morality Department of our police organization for years. The result is that we have no streets or section of the city given over to its accommodation. But it is true that there are some streets from which it is harder to keep it than from others. It is also true that there are notorious characters who have prematurely aged in the pursuit of vice and who, assisted by drink and associations, seem hopeless of reform. And, sadder still, it is true that every year there are scores and scores of young women ruined in this fair city. A sober estimate stated that 700 young women were cared for in the rescue homes of our city last year. If so large a number, many of whom are expectant mothers, were cared for in public institutions, how many must have been the cases of immoral conduct which never came to public attention at all.

4 The foreigner is with us, and here to stay. Whatever we may think of him as a neighbor, he is an economic necessity. With such great need for works of construction, as is realized in this new and rapidly-growing country, we must have his assistance. Many occupations have practically been deserted by our Anglo-Saxons, and the field is left to the 'Stranger within Our Gates.'

Perhaps, if we only knew the facts, the foreigner is a racial necessity.

Be these things as they may, here in our midst are 20,000 Jews, 7,000 Italians, 1,000 Chinamen, and Swedes, Macedonians, Russians, Greeks, and a variety of others, making a total of not less than 35,000. Many of these would feel insulted if told they need missionary endeavor. It is a well-known fact that the majority of these people have never known Christianity as we have learned it.

Some have known it only to curse it, while others, who have been reared nominally within its fold, have never known it as a personal experience of salvation and fellowship with God. Even had all these privileges been enjoyed before leaving the land of their birth, in the absence of spiritual shepherding, do we not need a new Pentecost, when at least the man who cannot understand our language shall be enabled to say to his fellows concerning the blessed Gospel, 'How hear we every man in our own tongue wherein we were born?'

5 Toronto is not without pauperism. Of the poor we have our share; of paupers, we sometimes fear we have more than our share. We distinguish a poor man from a pauper by the thought that the poor man, though living on meagre income, is yet not dependent, while 'the pauper is one who depends upon public or private charity for his sustenance.' The pauper works the public — the poor man works himself.

The ranks of pauperism are always being augmented from habits of drink and vice, whence come our vagrant men and women, and from the homes to which want has come, because of drunken fathers, husbands or mothers. In some cases the dependent is in no sense responsible for his state, as in the case of the class just named, or those whose earning power has been destroyed by disease, or injured by accidents which cripple and maim for life. In addition to all these, our most prolific source has been the English immigrant who has so long been nurtured under the parish relief systems of the old land, as were also his ancestors, that to him charity is always preferable to work, and appeals for help await only a good excuse. Then, too, there are not a few of these who see how keen the competition is which exists amongst religious and philanthropic organizations, where only co-operation ought to obtain, with the result that they are ever after the 'loaves and fishes.' Toronto has perhaps as many paupers of the latter class as any city of its size in America.

6 To speak of a slum in Toronto is to speak of a quantity not admitted by some of her citizens. But it is here, nevertheless, and has been for years. At a recent lecture in this city, given on 'Garden Cities and City Planning,' by Mr. H. Vivian, M.P., a series of slides furnished by our society, illustrating Toronto's slums, was thrown on the screen. Needless to say that the audience was shocked to think that our own fair city was harboring such conditions here.

Wretched housing conditions in Toronto

1 A by-way in the slums — notice the heaps of refuse
2 A rear view
3 The houses down the lane are the front view of no 4
4 Rear view of the houses
5 Not to be seen by the man on the street
6 The home of a peanut vendor

Several experts in housing, who have visited Toronto in recent months, have described our conditions as being as bad as anything in the Old Land. It is only fair to say that the extent of these conditions is comparatively limited, and it is only in the older sections of the city where these conditions are tolerated. We have houses in Toronto, in many of which is no plumbing or sanitary convenience, houses in which all decency and privacy are little regarded. Whole families live here in single rooms, and twenty boarders and a family may occupy a seven-roomed house and still keep out their sign, 'Board by day or week.' The continued neglect of such conditions on the part of our authorities would soon render certain sections extremely dangerous. But already light is dawning and the day, we trust, is at hand. To meet the moral needs and supply the deficiencies of the home under these conditions requires more than the religious indignation of better thinking people. While setting the municipal machinery in operation which shall improve the conditions, something must be done by somebody to provide facilities for social intercourse and to counteract the influence of the saloons and the playhouse upon such people. Children, too, must have some training and care, other than is to be found in this class of home. Hence the need for the institutional church or mission, and the social settlement.

To the Toronto City and Fred Victor Mission Society of the Methodist Church falls the responsibility of working among the classes referred to. Its work is distinct from that which any church is doing, and that not because of greater zeal, but because of greater facilities and constituted authority to do such work.

1 The headquarters and chief institution of the Society is the Fred Victor Mission, at the corner of Queen and Jarvis Streets.

2 In addition to that is The Italian Mission at 56 Elm Street, and its branch at 250 Claremont Street.

3 The Victor Home for young women at 266 Jarvis Street.

4 There is also The Victor Inn, an industrial institute for men, at 284 King Street East.

5 In the summer-time a gospel wagon works nightly on the street corners, and in the slums.

6 Down at the Union Station travellers will find representatives of the Traveller's Aid Department meeting, in co-operation with the representatives of the W.C.T.U., all in-coming and out-going trains.

The work of directing and helping the immigrant has also been entrusted to our Society.

7 And last, but not least, the Students' Campaign of Aggressive Evangelism.

One day's activities will suffice to illustrate the work. We will suppose it to be a winter day, when all departments are running.

We believe 'an ounce of prevention is worth a pound of cure.' Hence, everything possible is being done to interest and direct the minds of the children and young people. With reading room, gymnasium, manual training, and athletic clubs for the boys; for the girls, kitchen garden, gymnasium, cooking school, other branches of domestic science, junior and senior girls' clubs, sewing classes, elocution and Bible classes, there is something that appeals to all whom we can reach. By such agencies we seek to direct surplus energies in safe channels, and also to give training which will better fit for citizenship and home-builders. And we do not overlook the truly vital thing, the salvation of the soul. These agencies act as very good bait for the Gospel hook, so that in Bible classes and Sunday school, Sunday morning and evening children's services many are led to Christ and noble moral ideals.

The employment bureau in the inquiry office answers appeals for men to do odd jobs about the homes of the citizens, or a man may be wanted to go to the country to some farmer, or mayhap the inquiry is for female help, either of a temporary or permanent nature. In the case of the men, we send from our wood regiment, or family, applicants to fill these positions, and from lists always on file in the office women are furnished to those wishing help. The phone is not long idle. If it be not a call for help, it may be an order for wood, or some kind friend asking that our driver should call for a parcel, for clothing, or some needy, suffering creature may be seeking one of our deaconesses.

Meantime, across the hallway will be found one or other of the superintendents, answering correspondence or receiving calls from people in all manner of difficulty, and from all parts of the city. It may be the wife of some drunken husband, with whom she has borne as long as she possibly can, or the mother of a wayward boy, or perchance the husband of a deserting wife; or a heart-broken father, weary with the search for work which cannot be found, while hungry children await his home-coming, only to be disappointed; or perhaps some unfortunate victim of drink, who has lost his position

for the 'steenth time,' or some other poor fellow, 'down and out,'
with boots worn off his feet, and clothing disreputable. All these
people have to be helped with counsel or material aid, and that in
such a way that instead of being pauperized they must be elevated
and helped toward self-respect. On the walls of the office is our
motto, 'Charity is not our forte; we aim to help men to help
themselves.'

On Thursday afternoon at 2.30 mothers and children will be
found gathering in large numbers in the Assembly Hall. When all
have come you would see possibly one hundred and eighty or one
hundred and ninety mothers seated in groups of twelve or fifteen
around large tables. In the midst of each group is a worker, who
seeks to engage them in profitable conversation, and instruct in
simple or complicated sewing. The children, possibly sixty or
seventy of them, have been taken to a large room downstairs, where
they are entertained with kindergarten exercises by young ladies
from our best city homes. Upstairs, the proceedings for the afternoon have been opened with singing and prayer; and when an hour
has passed in sewing and conversation, the president will likely
introduce some leading pastor or Christian worker to address them
on some theme of domestic or Christian interest. Prior to this, however, three groups have been permitted to pass into the clothes-
room, where at merely nominal prices they obtain the clothing
which our friends so kindly send to us. The proceeds of this are
spent in supplying the refreshments which invariably follow the
address of the afternoon.

Besides this, supplies of new underwear, boots and shoes,
blankets and boys' clothing are kept on hand and are sold at prices
which defy the best 'bargain sales' of the stores. These are purchased
directly from the mills or jobbers and are sold at cost to those who
have the cash or who provide for payment by weekly payments in
advance.

This meeting is indeed a bright spot in the lives of these women,
some of whom work every day in the week but Thursday, and that
they sacredly reserve for this meeting. And no wonder, for each
worker tries to follow her mothers into their homes, and do all she
can to brighten their lives and lead them to Christ, if they are not
already converted. Through this agency many a heart is won for the
Saviour, and the integrity of many a home is preserved.

In connection with the mothers' meeting, a Fuel Club is operated, into which the members pay small sums each week in order that when winter comes, they may have their fuel paid for, as well as be able to buy it 25 to 50 cents a ton cheaper than elsewhere.

No sooner has this meeting dismissed than a small company of men appear, brooms in hand, to sweep the floor, after removing the tables, and prepare for the weekly 'free supper for homeless men.' This meeting starts at 7.30 p.m., but long before the hour the men will be found lined up out on the street waiting for the doors to open. As many as 450 men have crowded in on one night. These represent men from all walks of life — broken-down merchants, fallen professional men, degraded hoboes and occasionally men who have no stain upon their record, and have nothing worse against them than misfortune or lack of employment. The refreshments, consisting of a spiced loaf and large mug of steaming hot coffee, are now served by one of the Epworth Leagues of the city who provide this feast. Then follows a red hot evangelistic service, in which the address is usually given by the pastor, who accompanies the League. Then a fervent appeal is made, and sometimes a number will seek salvation. Many who now occupy good positions have been soundly converted, clothed and restored to their right mind by the influence of these meetings. And wherever the men scatter in the summer-time — on the farms, the lakes, into the woods, or in the alleys of the city — the influence of these services follows.

These are the special meetings of one day in the week. But while these are in progress, remember that two nurse deaconesses have been ministering to the suffering, whilst two other deaconesses have been visiting the homes, and dispensing Gospel truth and comfort wherever time and privilege permit. Any other day in the week than Thursday; the calendar shows a larger list of meetings and classes.

A savings bank is also operated here two nights each week where sums from two cents upwards may be deposited. Our branch is the pioneer of the Penny Bank of Canada now inculcating thrift and economy in the leading public schools of Toronto and Ontario.

In the summer-time the Gospel wagon carries its message of glad tidings to many who would never otherwise hear it. Sometimes the service is on the corner of a leading thoroughfare, where very many are passing to and fro. Sometimes the wagon finds its way down alleys and back streets, where numerous children play. Here wearied

mothers gather on the doorsteps or at the upstair windows, while the
men and the children gather about the wagon, and aid in the singing.
Ofttimes, with the truth of Gospel and song, they drink in conviction and salvation. Last year about ninety people confessed their
desire and purpose to lead new lives.

The Fred Victor Mission is a happy combination of activities
combining all the essential features of the Gospel Mission, the Institutional Church and the Social Settlement. For while the various
efforts indicated are put forth, the Associate Superintendent with
his family resides in the Mission buildings. Here also five of our
deaconesses reside in our 'Deaconess Settlement,' where their home
life is a centre of life and friendship to all the community.

As All Peoples' Mission, Winnipeg, differs from the Fred Victor
Mission, Toronto, in the character of the people whom it seeks to
help and also in some of its methods and ideals, we give a brief
summary of its work.

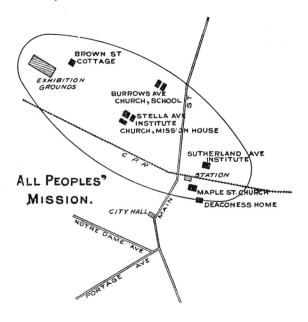

All Peoples' Mission geographically

I CONTROL
Methodist City Mission Board, Winnipeg.

II MANAGEMENT
An executive committee, working through
A *Standing committees* – (a) Finance; (b) State of the Work, (c) Extension.
B *Local boards of management* – (a) Maple St. (b) Bethlehem.

III SUPPORT
1 City Methodist churches
2 General Missionary Society
3 Woman's Missionary Society
4 Country churches
5 Individuals and societies
6 Winnipeg City grant

IV PLANT
A *Churches* (a) Maple Street; (b) Bethlehem; (c) Burrows Ave.
B *Institutes or neighborhood houses* (a) Sutherland Avenue Institute; (b) Stella Avenue Institute; (c) Burrows School; (d) Grand Theatre (rented during winter for Sunday meetings).
C *Homes* (a) Stella Avenue Mission House; (b) Maple Street Parsonage (Rented); (c) Deaconess Home (Deaconess Board).

   NB The Brown Street Branch was this year, at our request, taken over by an Anglican Church and has now developed into King Edward Settlement.

V STAFF
(a) The Superintendent,
(b) one ordained minister,
(c) eight deaconesses,
(d) three theological students,
(e) four kindergartners,
(f) one director boys' work,
(g) two students in training abroad,
(h) two young women in training,
(i) two caretakers,
(j) About 100 volunteer workers from Wesley College; Methodist churches and the city generally.

VI DEPARTMENTS

1 *Kindergarten* As yet, Winnipeg has no Kindergartens in connection with the public schools. In each Institute a largely attended morning and afternoon Kindergarten is maintained. These schools are especially needed among children who come from poor foreign homes, where the surroundings are not wholesome and where the mothers are frequently away at work during the day. These Kindergartens are 'feeders' to the public schools which, in the absence of a compulsory attendance law, the children must be induced to attend — after the parents have been pursuaded to allow them to do so! Further these kindergartens give access to several hundred homes that need help along almost every line.

2 *Girls' social and educational classes and clubs* The older children who are attending school or at work have many needs not provided for as yet by the community. So for some years we have maintained sewing classes, housekeeping classes, cooking classes and social clubs. Many of our girls work in factories or laundries and have few social opportunities in their own homes. The Institute aims to be for them something of a home, and to give them such ideals and training as will enable them to make good homes for themselves.

3 *Boys' social and educational classes and clubs* As manual training has been developing rapidly in the public schools it has not been deemed advisable to introduce this class of educational work. Considerable attention has been given to physical exercise in the gymnasium. In addition, there are games for the younger boys, and for the older boys social clubs in which are carried on debates, mock trials, etc. There are also several Boy Scout troops. The presence of women workers in the boys' rooms in the evenings gives something of the air of a home.

4 *Gymnasium and baths* are provided in both institutes for the boys and on certain evenings for the girls. There is close co-operation between the Mission, the Y.M.C.A. and the Playgrounds.

5 *Libraries* At each institute this is a branch of the City Public Library. The Institute workers are responsible for the care and distribution of the books. It is very gratifying to note the extensive use made of these libraries by children of foreign extraction.

6 *Night schools* A few years ago night schools were carried on much more extensively than at present. Since the opening of night schools by the Public School Board our classes have been confined

Glimpses of All Peoples' Mission, Winnipeg

1 Sutherland Avenue Institute
2 Immigrant women seeking advice from Deaconess
3 Stella Avenue Branch
4 A children's service

to a few special cases or have been carried on during the part of the
year when the city night classes were closed.

7 *Concerts and lectures* To provide wholesome entertainment and
instruction has seemed a matter of great importance. So in each
centre there are organized various series of popular lectures, illustrated talks, concerts, and entertainments of all kinds. While they
serve as a counter attraction to the cheap theatre, the dance hall and
the pool room, they are also valuable from an educational
standpoint.

8 *People's Sunday meetings* A recent development of the preceding department is the establishment of the People's Sunday
Meetings at the Grand Theatre. During the past season (Oct.,
1910 – March, 1911) this new venture met with somewhat remarkable success. In our constituency are large numbers of Jews,
Germans and Slavs and old-country working-men of radical views.
The English-speaking Protestant churches do not minister to these
classes and Sunday afternoon and evening is for them a time of no
special religious significance. The meetings were started with several
objects in view: (a) Providing a pleasant and profitable Sunday afternoon for many who had nowhere to go and nothing to do; (b)
Breaking down the racial, national, religious, political and social
prejudice that divide our heterogeneous population; (c) Placing
before these classes higher ideals. The afternoon meeting became
known as the 'People's Forum.' The lectures were chiefly on scientific, economic, and social subjects and were followed by free discussion. Representative people's leaders co-operated with the
committee in charge. The People's Sunday evening was not, in the
narrow sense of the term, a religious service. The ideal was rather
that of a Sunday evening at home – good music, beautiful pictures,
and conversational talks on helpful subjects. A *religious atmosphere*
was not lacking, the effect in part perhaps of the oft-repeated motto
'Thou shalt love the Lord thy God and thy neighbor as thyself.'
There were frequently three hundred men present in the afternoon
– once twelve hundred. In the evening the attendance grew steadily
till at the last meeting of the series the eight hundred mark was
reached. Jews and Russians, Catholics and Protestants, so-called
'Atheists,' Socialists and Christians found they could sit side by side
in a common enjoyment of the best things in life and unite in spirit
as they considered the things that made for the common welfare.

9 *Women's meetings* Mothers' Meetings and Women's Clubs are organized to draw the women of various nationalities into helpful associations.

10 *Men's associations* A Ruthenian Temperance Society, a Bohemian Club, 'Komensky,' and various other societies have been encouraged to organize the rooms provided in which their meetings could be held.

11 *Relief* Considerable relief is given in the course of the year, though since the formation of the Associated Charities this has been largely confined to immediate relief, clothing, delicacies, and Christmas cheer.

12 *Friendly visiting* One of our deconesses acts as a 'friendly visitor' for the Associated Charities. Nearly all the workers do more or less of this kind of work in connection with their particular departments.

13 *Hospital visiting* There being no hospital chaplain, a mission worker regularly visits the General Hospital.

14 *Immigration chaplaincy* The minister stationed at Maple St. Church acts as Methodist Immigration Chaplain, having an office in the Immigration Hall, where during the spring months he spends most of his time meeting the immigrants.

15 *Religious services* There are two organized congregations: (a) Maple Street, the 'mother' mission, composed largely of recently arrived 'Old Country' people, serves as an immigration chapel, and attempts to reach the men living in the cheap hotels and boarding houses in the vicinity. It maintains weekly prayer meetings, Epworth League, and temperance society. (b) Bethlehem, opened as a Slavic Mission, is now organized as an English-speaking church, the members being mostly English Methodists. A Protestant Bohemian service is still conducted on Sunday mornings. Weekly cottage prayer meetings are held. (c) There are English-speaking services for adults and for children in the two Institutes and in Burrows School. These buildings have also been used by Russian Baptists and a congregation of Syrians. (d) For the past two years the use of Burrows Avenue Church has been granted to the former owners, a congregation of the Polish National Catholic Church. (e) Four Sunday Schools are maintained.

16 *Co-operation with other social agencies* This is probably the most important department of our work. The public schools, the

health department, the Associated Charities, the Children's Aid, the
Fresh Air work of the Deaconess Board — with these, and a score
more similar organizations, we are in the most intimate touch. We
regard them as *part of our work* and aid them as far as lies in our
power.

The Superintendent of the Mission serves on the Boards of a
number of City 'Charities' and social organizations, and is, this year,
a member of the City Playground Commission and the Manitoba
Government Commission on Technical education.

17 *Investigation* The mission workers have at various times
undertaken several small investigations of local social conditions.
Before effective remedies can be applied the disease must be studied
and its cause determined.

18 *Publicity* To bring social needs to the attention of the public
has been a necessary part of our work. This has involved interviews,
correspondence, addresses, newspaper articles, reports, books, etc.

19 *Training workers* Social workers are not easily procured. In
fact many of our problems are so recent that we have few ready to
deal with them. This has necessitated to a certain degree the training
of our own workers.

20 *Assisting other churches* During the past year we have been
able to 'loan' workers to other churches who felt the need of starting
institutional work.

21 *An experimental station* The value of many forms of social
work must be locally demonstrated before they are adopted by the
community. In several matters we have been able to do pioneer
work, present as it were an object lesson, and finally have had the
satisfaction of helping to promote a permanent organization or
institute a new public department. Where this is established, we can
unload and tackle something else.

Our policy is flexible and is the practical working out of our
Watchwords:

1 First things first.
2 Thy Kingdom come.
3 Lord, open our eyes!
4 Idealize the Real; realize the Ideal.
5 Not to be ministered unto but to minister.
6 All things to all men.
7 Supply real needs.

8 Fill the vacant niche.
9 Do it now.
10 Stay with it.
11 Prevention better than cure.
12 Organized helpfulness.

How can I help? In studying the foregoing detailed descriptions each reader will already have found something that he can do. Begin by trying to meet the nearest need. That need reveals one still deeper and soon you reach a great social problem. Work at that and the whole field of social service opens up to you. Help effectively one man and you lift the world.

As organizations, along what lines should we advance? Our study ought to have shown us the unlimited latent possibilities in our existing social institutions. Our ideal ought to be not to create new organizations but rather to really socialize those already in existence — that is, when they are capable of being socialized, otherwise to relegate them to the scrap heap.

Take, for instance, our Public Schools. There is no good reason why the scope of the work of our schools should not be extended to include much, if not all, of the work now carried on by the settlements and institutional churches and missions. So with many other municipal and State departments. They are machines to serve the people. Let good people — the best people — work them.

Ah, there's the rub! The majority of our citizens do not yet realize the opportunities or feel the responsibilities of citizenship. Here is an exhortation from that veteran social leader, Dr. Washington Gladden:

The sacredness, the solemnity of these obligations of citizenship, the Church must somehow manage to impress on the minds of all the people. It must make the people in the pews see and feel that their refusal to take part in the government of the city, the state and the nation is nothing other than a flagrant breach of trust. It must drive home to the consciences of these thrifty citizens the truth that they have no right to refuse public office, be it ever so inconspicuous or laborious; that when the commonwealth calls them they must not say: 'I pray thee have me excused.' 'Too busy.' A man might as well say, 'I am too busy to pay my note at the bank, or to provide food

for my household.' No moral obligation can outrank our duty
to the commonwealth, for on the maintenance of good government
everything that we hold dear in the world depends – our lives, our
property, the security of our homes, the possibility of sound manhood and womanhood for our children. Here, if anywhere, is the
central obligation of social morality, and the man who shirks it must
be made to feel that his defalcation exposes him to the wrath of God
and the scorn of man.

We can hardly be accused of under-estimating the value of social
settlements, institutional churches, and city missions, but more and
more we are convinced that such agencies will never meet the great
social needs of the city. They serve a present need; they bring us face
to face with our problem; they point out the line of advance. Then
by all means let us multiply them and extend the scope of their
work. But the needs will remain until the community at large is
dominated by the social ideal.

This surely is the mission of the Church, and yet the Church itself
is hardly awake to the situation, much less fitted to meet it. Will the
Church retain – perhaps we should rather say, regain – her social
leadership?

'We have seen,' says Rauschenbusch,

that the crisis of society is also the crisis of the Church. The
Church, too, feels the incipient paralysis that is creeping upon our
splendid Christian civilization through the unjust absorption of
wealth on one side and the poverty of the people on the other. It
cannot thrive when society decays. Its wealth, its independence, its
ministry, its social hold, its spiritual authority, are threatened in a
hundred ways.

But on the other hand the present crisis presents one of the
greatest opportunities for its growth and development that have ever
been offered to Christianity. The present historical situation is a high
summons of the Eternal to enter upon a larger duty and thereby to
inherit a larger life.

If rightly directed, a little effort in this time of malleable heat will
shape humanity for good more than huge labor when the iron is
cold. If Christianity would now add its moral force to the social and
economic forces making for a nobler organization of society, it

could render such help to the cause of justice and the people as would make this a proud page in the history of the Church for our sons to read. And in turn the sweep and thrill of such a great cause would lift the Church beyond its own narrowness. If it would stake its life in this cause of God, it would gain its life. If it follows the ways of profit and prudence, it will find its wisdom foolishness. At the beginning of the modern foreign missionary movement the Church was full of timid scruples about its call and its ability for such a work. To-day there are few things in the life of the Church which so inspire its finest sons and daughters and so intensify the Christ-spirit in its whole body as this movement in which it seems to scatter its strength abroad. If the social movement were undertaken in a similar spirit of religious faith and daring, it would have a similar power to re-christianize the Church.

'Re-christianize the Church' – mark the phrase. It .is worth thinking over. May we not be on the eve of a great social and religious reformation? Within and without the church do we not feel the stirrings of the new life – yes, it is coming!

In a recent article in *The Survey* (March 4th, 1911) Prof. Graham Taylor gives a sweeping review of recent movements within the Church in which he shows that the Church is *'preparing for social action.'* The report of our own General Conference Committee on Sociological questions is most significant and inspiring. We give several extracts:

We believe the Master has intended that in industrial, commercial and political affairs, in laws and social regulations, and in the spirit of all our dealings with each other the principles of the Golden Rule and the Sermon on the Mount should govern. Only through these can we be led out of our semi-barbaric commercialism, and only by means of these can we lay firm and strong the foundations of the Kingdom of God upon earth ...

This co-partnership of men in a community is the basis of many other duties also. If an individual amasses wealth, it is the community which gives him the opportunity ... The community is, therefore, part owner of the wealth ...

We acknowledge with regret that the present social order is far from being an ideal expression of Christian brotherhood. We deplore the great evils which have their source in the commercial greed of our times which often leads men to oppress the unfortunate and to forget their obligations to the higher interests of society.

We deplore these existing economic conditions which tend to accentuate the inequality of opportunity open to the various classes of the community and to permit through artificial unfair conditions the amassing of the larger proportions of the wealth of the country in the hands of the few with all the attendant economic social and political dangers.

In the presence of these and other evils, the church of Christ cannot stand inactive and silent. We truly express our sympathy with all those who suffer from unjust economic conditions, by making most sincere efforts to find practical solutions of the insistent problems of our industrial life. We regard as our brothers-in-arms all who in organized form or otherwise are struggling for justice for themselves and for others. We regard man's cause as God's cause always and everywhere ...

Surely social workers ought to thank God and take courage!

We conclude with a ringing message from Dr. Frank Mason North, Secretary of the New York City Extension and Missionary Society of the Methodist Episcopal Church and editor of *The Christian City:*

The Christian faith confronts a new civilization. Whatever its conquest in the heathen world, the gospel will have won its complete triumph only when it has tamed the mighty forces itself has freed and has brought them into obedience to Jesus Christ.

It is a new civilization, new in its material basis, in its industry, in its social order, in its intellectual viewpoint, in its religious concepts. Influences are at work which are changing the face, if not the heart, of the world. A crisis for the individual and society is created which lifts these early years of the twentieth century to the level of the great epochs — the invasion of Gothic hordes, the crusades, the revival of learning, the discovery of printing and of a continent. Wise men are silenced not alone by the complexity, but by the unexpectedness of their problems. Heroism to-day meets not only the tests of courage, but of surprise. Faith confronts the civilization not of a hundred — of fifty — of ten — years ago, but a civilization strange, ardent, expectant, progressive and in its progress listening for the new call from above — eager for the new spirit which shall inform and master it.

Of this new civilization the city is the centre. The forces of nature, trained to service, converge upon it. The materials and methods of industry command it. The confluence of nations is at its gate. To it learning brings its problems; in its libraries and universities, in its treasures of art and of science, finds its resources; in the attrition and concentration of the city becomes conscious of its power and its mission. The city is the test and the opportunity of mind. In the city the problems of the social order become acute, and there reach the beginnings of their solution. What a man is — in his rights, in his aims, in his equipment; what he owns, his labor, his property, his reputation; what the community asks of him in personal and property surrender, in sacrifice of privilege, of direct service for the commonwealth; under what laws — natural or artificial — the quest for bread, the conduct of trade, the education of childhood, the maintenance of the home, are to be guaranteed; how he is to be free though governed, and governed though free; how out of racial friction the personal life shall survive; how he shall be his own and his brother's keeper, and shall find the Master's answer to the question, 'Who is my neighbor?' — these are the social problems of the world, condensed, defined, formulated, vitalized in the life of the city.

Here religion finds its test, its travail, its triumph. Can the gospel be commercialized? The city will give reply. Is there power in spiritual motive to deal with materialism, with goods, with recreation, with luxury? The city is the final test. Do truth and righteousness belong to the realm of fancy, or are they the pillars of human society, of the home, of the community, of organized government? The ultimate demonstration is in the city. Has Jesus Christ a place among men — not alone for blessed walks with disciples in quiet roadways, but for breaking bread for hungry multitudes? Let the city answer. The city is more than the hotbed of revolution; it is the fiery furnace for the test of faith; it is more than the hope of Democracy, as one has recently called it; it is the ultimate arena of the successive conflicts of the Christian faith with the power of the world.

If the new civilization is to be mastered by Christ, the city must be taken for Him.

REFERENCES

'Guide to Reading on Social Ethics and Allied Subjects'
Cambridge, Mass.: Harvard University
'The New Encyclopedia of Social Reform'
W. D. P. Bliss. New York: Funk, Wagnalls Co.
Publications of the American Institute of Social Service, Fourth
Avenue, near 23rd St., New York
Publications League of Progressive Thought and Social Service,
27 Chancery Lane, London, W.C.
Publications Department of Church and Labor, Presbyterian
Church, U.S.A., 156 Fifth Ave., New York
Publications of the Methodist Federation for Social Service.
New York: Eaton & Mains
Publications Wesleyan Methodist Union for Social Service.
London: Robert Culley
New Bibliography of Settlements. Russell Sage Foundation,
New York

In addition to books previously mentioned:
'Jesus Christ and the Social Question'
F. G. Peabody. New York: The Macmillan Co.
'The Gospel and the Modern Man'
Shailer Mathews. New York: The Macmillan Co.
'Social Solutions in the Light of Christian Ethics'
T. C. Hall. New York: Eaton & Mains
'The Social Basis of Religion'
Simon N. Patten. New York: The Macmillan Co.